ALBERT ERHART HARTWIG

THIS IS MY STORY AND I'M STICKING TO IT !

As told by: Del Hartwig

Pictures submitted by Del Hartwig

ISBN-10: 1517145341
ISBN-13: 978-1517145347

DEDICATION

I lovingly dedicate this book to my husband Al,
a man I admire, respect and love. I thank God
everyday that this wonderful man chose me to
share his life and love with.

Del

CONTENTS

ACKNOWLEDGEMENTS

I want to take a moment to thank my husband for answering all of my questions concerning his younger years and his life prior to me. I also want to thank him, for taking over and doing the chores that I usually handle, laundry, house work, dishes and sometimes even the cooking. Without his love and help, this story would not have been possible.

A thank you to Doug Walker, who showed me several "tricks" to using the computer and to adding "the Drop-Box" feature so that Al could more easily proof read the book for me.

A Big Thank you, to our granddaughter, Jessica Moore for helping me put all of the information on a USB stick (which I had absolutely no idea of how to do).

I also want to give a special Thank You, to Dr. John Wiens, who spent many hours and days helping me to get this book published.

FORWORD

I have always been an avid book reader and have been writing poetry for years, but I have never written a book before. While I was at the hair salon this one day, I got talking with a woman about some of our experiences being up in northern Manitoba. One of the stylists suggested that I should write a story about the experiences I had while I and my husband owned a fly-in fishing camp on Gods Lake.

I thought about it, and was first of all going to write a story about myself as had been suggested. Then I got to thinking, my husband, Al had had many more adventures than I ever had, and I would also have a small part of his story.

So I started asking Al some questions regarding his life before he met me. After a lot of asking, he finally started to talk and tell me stories about his previous life.

This story is for all of those people who know him, or think they know him, or think they know about him.

Also, I have written this for our four children, grandchildren and those great, great grandchildren who may someday want to know about their grandfather, what his life was like and what he did.

I want people to know the kind of man he is honest, ethical, moral and very loving. This story is also about his life and experiences both before and after we were married.

Our life has been one Great Adventure and I look forward to having many more years to enjoy with this wonderful man; and I sincerely hope that I have been able to tell his story well enough, that those who are reading this will get to know him as I do; a wonderful, interesting, funny, warm and loving man I know, respect and love.

Del Hartwig

THAT KIND of MAN

(A Tribute to My Husband)

I knew you were special
the first time we
met
And though time has brought
changes, I'll never
forget.

All the sweet things you've done
All the "firsts" that we've
shared.
All the times I've been happy
just knowing you
cared.

As the years have passed I've
loved seeing you
grow,
As a husband, a father,
a friend people
know,

They can count on to help
any way that he
can,

I'm proud to be married to
that kind of
man.

By: Del Hartwig

PREFACE

In the beginning......

All good stories start this way, so I guess I'll do the same. There is a story or "legend" regarding some of my ancestors. Now I will not claim that this is true, but this is what has been passed down.

The story is that there were some Hartwig brothers who were ship owners and who brought a shipload of Hessian soldiers over to America back in the 1700's. When the young Hartwigs were not able to collect the passage money that was promised to them for the mercenaries, the brothers decided to do a little exploring on their own and they sailed up the lower St. Lawrence River and headed west through the Great Lakes.

They were supposed to have stopped in what is now Fort Francis, Ontario for awhile; and finally made their way to what later became Milwaukee and eventually settled in the Port Washington area.

Like I said, I cannot say for sure that this story is true or not, but I can tell you that my grandfather, Dr. Theodore Hartwig did sail over to America from Germany in 1846; and he actually did settle in Cedarburg, Wisconsin where he met and married my grandmother, Caroline Hodan.

He was the only doctor in that area and he and his wife raised five children, one of whom was my father, Albert T. Hartwig. My father was the only one, of my grandparent's three sons who did not become a doctor, but he did a lot of other things; including going west, finding a silver mine and then using the money he made from the mine, bought a brewery in Eau Claire, Wisconsin, which got burned down by the Suffragettes.

e then moved back to Cedarburg where he raised prize Morgan horses, im-
ted English Springer Spaniels and Irish Setter dogs, as well as a couple of
r breeds. He also owned a tavern called "Five Corners" because it was in
iddle of five roads. Cedarburg is where he met and married my mother,
e of his life when he was sixty-three years old and they lived happily until
h, and I guess, this is where my story begins......

Albert Erhart Hartwig—THIS IS MY STORY AND I'M STICKING TO IT!

By: My Wife, Del Hartwig

Chapter One

Baby Steps and My Motor's Running

I was born on February 10, 1929 in Cedarburg, Wisconsin, U.S.A., at 11:45 am. to Marie Magdalena Erhart Hartwig, 37 years old and to Albert Theodore Hartwig, 67 years old. My father's occupation was listed as "store proprietor" and my mother as "housewife". Actually, the "store" was a tavern/store/boarding house and is still there in Cedarburg today, but it is under a new name. I was told, that my mother the morning I was born, had prepared breakfast for their 14 boarders, washed clothes and hung them on the line to dry; then assisted by my father gave birth to me on a table in the tavern area in front of the bar. She then made dinner and had it on the table for their boarders when they came in that night. Boy, now that's what I call a "woman"! The next day my father called a doctor to come by and "retie" the string around my umbilical cord, as my father had cut the "cord" too short and the string had come untied. The doctor also recorded my birth at that time.

Now I know that this may sound a little strange, but I can really remember being born! I remember feeling warm and happy one moment and the next feeling a terrible pressure and pain. This seemed to go on a very long time and then all at once I found myself hanging upside down and feeling like I was freezing. I can also remember laying in my crib not be-

Figure 1: My parents in the 1920's with a friend. My Dad is the very tall man on the left.

Figure 2: A view of my parent's tavern where I was born

ing able to move or roll over; so I would cry, holler and fuss until this very nice lady would come in, speak to me and turn me over so that I could see the many pretty colored things hanging over my head on top of the crib. For awhile I was happy and contented with this, but then I finally got bored and the process of crying, hollering and fussing would start all over again.

Figure 3: The inside of my parent's tavern,
Dad is behind the bar. I was born on one of
the tables.

One day, I discovered that I could get around by myself by crawling. Wow, was that great! Now each day became a new adventure. I do not know exactly how old I was, but I hadn't started walking yet. My mother put me into a walker, (this is a seat with side rails to hold the child, and wheels so that when the child puts their feet on the floor, they are able to move around from place to place). This was one of the Best days of my life, I could "travel" all around the place and not have to remain in one spot all the time, or hurt my neck trying to see where I was going when I crawled. Then one day, as fate would have it, I was in my walker and scooting all over, I came racing around the corner of the door-way (I felt like I was going as fast as the wind!) well, as I got into the kitchen I discovered that someone had forgotten to close the door to the basement, of course I didn't have any brakes and couldn't stop fast enough, so I went "flying" down the basement stairs into the coal-bin. I didn't get hurt, thank goodness, just shaken up a bit but I can tell you I was never so scared in my entire life!

The day finally came when I was able to stand on my own two feet, (of course I was a bit wobbly and had to hold on to the sofa for a little help), but I could stand! It made me feel proud like I had really done something great! I can remember my father sitting in his chair with his hands out trying to convince me to walk over to him. Now you have to remember, to do this, I would have to let go of the sofa and it seemed like a REAL-LY LONG way over there. But I finally got my "Dutch Courage," u enough to let go of the sofa and tried to do as my father asked. Of course I have to say it did take several tries to finally reach him but I did it, and on my own two feet. Wow, congratulations, way to go Al !!

A couple of years later I was given a baby brother; and one incident which stands out in my mind, is about this one Sunday morning as my mother was getting us ready to go to church. She had just gotten us all dressed to go, both my brother and me. I was dressed in a little red-velvet "romper" (this is an outfit with short cut off pants) style suit.

Ma had to change my baby brother, Carl's diaper and she set me on the kitchen counter and told me to sit still. I did as I was told but as I was sitting there waiting for my mother to finish changing Carl's diaper, I found a fountain pen and picked it up to examine it. I was very intrigued with this strange thing, it had a long round rubber tube that was filled with a black liquid (I didn't know then, but it was ink), and I soon had taken it apart, the better to figure out what it was and how it worked.

I then heard my mother coming back and I very quickly tried to put the

4

"thing" (pen) back together before she found me. Needless to say, I wasn't quick enough and she discovered me all covered in black ink. I have to say she wasn't pleased with me, and that would be an understatement! I do not remember if I ever wore that red velvet suit again.

Because my parents had a business to run, as I got older (pre-school age) I would sometimes "sneak" out on my own to discover and explore my world, and this did not always just include my own back yard. I was never bad or destructive, just curious. One day I discovered the water tower in our town; it had a ladder on the side that went all the way to the top. I wondered if I could see the whole world from up there, so I climbed up to have a look. Oh the view, it was spectacular, the whole town lay out there below me. I bet if I looked hard enough I would be able to see all the way to the bottom of the world! I was so intrigued by the view from up there that I went back several times and climbed the water tower. Well, one day after I had again climbed to the top of the tower to have a look around, I happened to spot a police car parked on the street below me. It stayed there for quite a long time, actually it stayed until it was getting dark and I knew I had better be getting home soon. But because the police car was parked down below, I was afraid to climb down and have him see me. So I stayed up there awhile longer.

Finally, the police car drove away and I proceeded to hurry and climb down from the tower so I could go home. As I reached the bottom, the police chief grabbed me, handcuffed and took me back to the police station where I was finger printed and put in a cell and there given bread and water. He told me, "that this is what they do to people who do things they are not supposed to do". I was so scared! I eventually heard my father's voice pleading with the police chief to let me go and promising that I would never do that again. It was sure good to hear him and I can honestly say that this is the only time I have ever been in trouble with the law or in jail. In later years, I found out that the police chief had talked to my father, who was a city council member and told him about my climbing up the water tower. My father told him to give me a good scare. Well boy, that police chief sure did what he was told!

The only other time I remember doing something "illegal", was when I accompanied my mother shopping at a "Five and Ten Cent" store (today we would probably call them a Dollarama Store), while I followed her around, I saw some candy that I wanted and asked her for it she said, "No". So while she wasn't looking I took the three pieces of candy I wanted and put them into my pocket. When we returned home and she discovered the candy she very harshly scolded me for stealing. My father however called the manager of the store and told him what I had done, and that they were going to bring me back to the store so I could "confess my crime" of stealing the three pieces of candy.

When I got to the store the next morning, the store manager pretended that he didn't know what I was going to tell him. I stood before this man and told him how I had taken the three pieces of candy and had put them into my pocket without paying for them. The manager then reprimanded me very severely and called me a thief. I felt so ashamed and to this day I have never taken nor stolen anything that did not belong to me. It was a lesson I never forgot.

Oh yes, before I forget, I better tell you about another of my escapades. Right behind our back yard were mink pens owned by Fromm Brothers Mink Farms, who raised both mink and fox, they would sell the skins to furriers, who would make the skins into fur coats and hats, which were very popular with the public to wear at that time. Well they kept rabbits under the pens just in case the mink happened to get loose they would go after the rabbits instead of just running away. I really wanted to catch one of those cute little bunnies, so I used the fold-up stairs the owner used to climb over the fence to get into the mink pens to take care of them. I used that same means to get in there by the rabbits and had a great time chasing those bunnies. Needless to say again, my parents were not too pleased with me because if the mink would have gotten out I could have been badly hurt.

When I was four years old, the Chicago World's Fair opened, it was called: A Century of Progress International Exposition, but everyone just called it, the Chicago World's Fair. This was in 1933 and lasted until 1934. As I mentioned, my parents took my little two year old brother Carl and me to see it, after all Milwaukee is only eighty (80) miles from Chicago, and boy, was it exciting.

Two things that I remember best about going to the Fair, was seeing the German airship the Graf Zeppelin and a belly dancer named "Little Sheba", hey, she had a big red ruby in her belly button, can you imagine that? Yeah, a big bright red ruby, what's not to remember?

I also remember going inside of a "Blimp". I was watching with my parents all the people going on this big "Blimp", when suddenly I found myself in line with a lot of other people. I was too small to see my parents, but I was sure they were right behind me. So I just kept moving forward and soon found myself "attached" to a large family with a lot of children. I stayed real close and went inside with them, it was Awesome! It was really something to see. My parents, of course were not pleased with me again as they were frantically looking all over for me. When they saw me, I got a harsh punishment for taking off on my own.

Also around the time I was about five or a little bit more, our older half brother Max, had built a boat, called a Lapstrake boat, which is a nice fishing type boat."

One day, my brother Carl, who is younger than me, and myself needed a "clubhouse" (you know a fort, or playhouse) that sort of thing. When we spotted Max's new boat, it looked "pretty good" to us, and we decided that it would make a perfect place for our "fort".

The ONLY thing it needed was a door, (the boat was upside down and we could not get under it). So Carl and I got one of our father's saws, and proceeded to "cut a door" in the side of the boat.

BOY, Let Me Tell You, Max did not appreciate our efforts or resourcefulness !!!

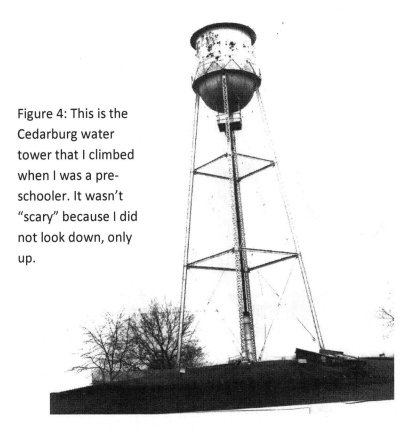

Figure 4: This is the Cedarburg water tower that I climbed when I was a pre-schooler. It wasn't "scary" because I did not look down, only up.

Chapter Two

On the Apron, Waiting to Taxi

When I started grade one in school, (they didn't have kindergarten then) I was unable to speak any English only German. My parents were both German and all of their friends and relatives were German and that was the only language they all spoke. So when I got to school I became both puzzled and upset as I could not understand what anyone at school was saying. When my parents found out, they were shocked about this and decided to start speaking only English at home so that I would be able to speak and understand what other people were saying. So from that day forward my parents never spoke another word of German to me. But by the end of that school year I was the best speller in the "Spelling-Bee in my class, and the word which won that title for me was, "teacher".

The year I was six and in grade one, my parents moved to Milwaukee, Wisconsin U.S.A. so my mother could be closer to her brothers who had come over from Germany to be cheese makers. Our first home there was across from the famous Aster Hotel where many Hollywood celebrities and other well known personalities would stay. Our house number was twelve thirty-four Aster Street. But I learned to remember our house number by 1, 2, 3, 4 Aster, and I never forgot my home address

When we arrived in Milwaukee, my parents bought a restaurant and my mother operated it, my father was quite ill by this time. It was the time of the Great Depression, many people were out of work and people were not able to afford to eat out much in restaurants as they had been doing in the 1920's, so my parents had to close the doors, and my mother's brothers went back to Germany as well around this time.

Even in my young years I would try to help out. I did this by helping to clean a three floor rooming house on weekends and summer holidays for

Figure 5: The old Police Station and Fire Hall in Cedarburg, If you look real close, you can probably still see the "bars" on the windows. This is the only "jail" I have ever been in.

Figure 7: This is a picture of a Lapstrake boat, and is similar to the boat my brother Max built and which I and Carl cut a "door" in for our clubhouse.

twenty-five cents per day. After working for two days I earned myself a grand total of fifty cents. With this grand sum of money I could buy: a pound of butter, a dozen eggs and a quart of milk and I would have five cents left over so I could buy an ice cream cone, this was my "treat" or reward I guess you could say, but the food that I was able to purchase helped my family.

Sometime, I guess, oh about grade two or three, I was having a real hard time learning to read (maybe I spent too much time looking out the window and day-dreaming) anyway, the teacher complained to my parents regarding my inattention, so my older half-brother, Max (he was twelve years older than me) spent a whole weekend teaching me to read. When I arrived at school on Monday morning, my teacher again called on me to read aloud. I did, while looking out the window and holding my book upside down! The teacher finally figured out that I was actually reciting the book from memory, all because Max had worked so long teaching me to read, I guess I had memorized the whole book.

One of my best friends during my school days was Ray Stuiber. Ray and I were about the same age and we enjoyed many childhood adventures and secrets together. I will tell you about one of them. We were probably around eight or nine at the time and lived near old St. John's Cathedral, well this church had sustained a fire, the interior had been gutted and the church had just started having it repaired. There was scaffolding all over the place, Ray and I thought that the bell tower would make a great secret club house, so we climbed the stairs as far as they went and then grabbed the bell tower rope and climbed that to the top. (I even carved my initials up there). This bell tower was about six stories high.

Sometime during that summer, Ray and I decided to go to our secret club house again up in the bell tower during the night. So we snuck out of doors and headed for St. John's. We climbed up to the top of all the scaffolding and took turns daring each other to follow one another on the planks, using our toes as guides. We left after we had come to the end of a plank where there seemed to be nothing but empty space at the end of it and we could go no further. I guess our Guardian Angels were with us that night or we had been very lucky, because this was the only time that Ray had waited back at the beginning of the plank instead of being right behind me as we had been doing all night. The next day when we went back and looked up at the scaffolding we had walked on the night before, (it was over four stories up), and we saw that the last plank we had been walking on was sticking out over the end of the scaffolding about four feet. I guess I don't have to tell you that Ray and I never tried that stunt again. But hey, we were boys, young and adventurous, so what can I say?

In 1939, the movie "The Wizard of Oz" came out in the movie theatres, this was one of the first colored movies to be shown. I was around nine years old and my brother Carl was around seven. The cost to see this movie was thirty-five cents per person (it was 'big bucks" back in those days) usually it was only ten cents per person but because as I mentioned before, this was the first colored movie so it cost more. Anyway we worked the whole summer collecting paper and brass from old broken light bulbs and old rags and hauled it all the way from the town dump in a coaster (a metal wagon) one and a half miles to the nearest junk dealer who would buy this "stuff". He, the junk dealer, however, would only pay us half of what it was worth because we were kids. He told us to take what he offered or we could haul our coaster another mile and a half to another junk dealer. (This one would have paid us honestly for what we had brought to him).

After working that hard to get the stuff, having the hobos throw garbage and other things at us and chase us away so we were not able to get at the easier stuff, we decided to take the "deal".

Back then for instance, used old paper was worth around four cents for a hundred pounds, so if you were only making two cents for a hundred pounds, it wasn't very much money that you got for all of your hard work. But we finally made enough money to see the movie which was shown at the Riverside Theatre in downtown Milwaukee and thoroughly enjoyed every minute of it.

When I was eleven, my father died and I learned to grow up pretty fast, and I virtually became the "head" of our family and had to help support them.

Speaking of my dad, I remember he was a big man with very big hands, hands that were so big, that he would pick me up by the top of my head, turn me around to face him and look me in the eye when he talked to me if I had been misbehaving when I was younger. I also remember the dogs my father had. He bred and raised pedigreed Springer Spaniels and other hunting breeds, and would only sell them to the persons he felt would be able to bond and take care of them. In fact my first pet was one of dad's dogs. His name was "Freckles". I do not know how old he was or how long we had him as I was very young at the time. But I do remember playing with Freckles.

Figure 8: "Freckles" my dog is on the right. The other dog is a Water Spaniel hunting dog of my Dad's.

Another thing I remember concerning my dad, was how he and his friends would get together every day and play a card game called, "Sheepshead." Dad taught me how to play when I was just a little guy, oh I guess I was around four or maybe five years old, but I would take the place of one of the men if he had to leave the game to go to the washroom or something. I guess I got pretty good when I was young, but I sure have no idea how to play the game now.

Another thing I remember my father did was, he would set me up on his bar as he attended taking care of his customers. He did this while my mother was working getting the meals ready or what-ever; anyway he would take care of looking after me while my mother was busy. When I was sitting up there, he would give me a "shot" glass of beer and all the pretzels I could eat. It kept me entertained and out of mischief, where he could watch me and take care of business at the same time. You know, I still like pretzels even now when I drink beer.

So okay, after my mother lost the restaurant and just before my father died, we had to go on what was called "Relief", today we call it welfare, but at that time it was known as "Relief". When you were on "Relief", you did not receive any money as you do today, instead you would receive what was called "commodities". For instance, a family of four would receive: about a pound of split dried peas, a pound of dried beans, a pound of lard, a pound of sugar, three cans of milk, ten pounds of flour, yeast, ten pounds of elbow macaroni, and two pounds of salt pork with the hair sticking out of the rind, but nothing fresh. During this time, I would go to the dumpsters behind the grocery stores, where I would find over ripe fruit and vegetables. When you got rid of the bad parts, you could have fresh fruit and vegetables to eat.

Also, I would go to the butcher shops and they would give me bones free, (as they were just thrown away in those days), so that I could take them home for my mother to make soup with. I would also catch crayfish and smelt (a kind of fish which is small like a sardine) which my mother cooked for us and made a nice change from the "commodities". I and my brother Carl would catch crayfish, (these are small lobster like looking things), in the lagoon which was in Juneau Park. The lagoon was about two hundred feet wide and one half mile long located between Lake Michigan shore line and a road going through the park.

To catch crayfish, you would take a small one inch piece of liver, (which you could get free from the butcher shop), tie it to a piece of string and "hang" it into the shallow water in the lagoon, after a few minutes, you would slowly "pull" the string up to the water surface and hold a strainer under it to catch the crayfish as they dropped off. When you had a large pail filled you would take it home, soak them in salt water to clean them out and then boil them in fresh salted water and eat them, they tasted a little like lobster." They are just small, so you had to have a lot of them for a meal.

Then my mother bought me my first bike. It was a Schwinn from Sears and Roebuck, the cost was twenty four dollars and ninety five cents. My mother would pay one dollar and fifty cents each month for it out of her "Mother's Pension". I rode that bike all year long and it took me all over, even to my job each morning and evening.

I really was getting somewhere now!

Figure 9: Pictures of me as a young boy. I guess I could always find something to do.

Figure 10: A picture of myself and my two brothers. Max is the oldest, then me (I'm in the middle) and Carl, the "baby". This is one of the few pictures of the three of us together.

Chapter Three

Airplanes and Youthful Hi-Jinks

One of the most embarrassing moments that I can remember, is when I was around the age of nine years old. We were living on Kilbourn Street in Milwaukee, Wisconsin at this time. I must have been extremely tired, because I "sleep-walked", the first and only time in my life; but when I woke up, I was several blocks from home and I didn't have any clothes on. I was "stark naked", yikes!

 When I reached home, the police were waiting for me; my mom and dad had found me missing and my window open, so they had immediately called the police. I have to say, I was really very embarrassed.

Another time, I and Ray, my best friend, were curious as to what happened at the Arthur Murray Dance School. So we ran over there and of course we were too small to reach the fire escape stairs but there was an awning right below with a rope and a pipe that was holding the awning. We climbed the rope up to the pipe until we reached the fire escape stairs, which had an open door that led into a small "cloak room" with a lot of coats hanging up, and a light "switch" on the wall.

After looking inside, we saw a whole room full of people dancing. Ray and I thought that we would "play" a joke on the people who were dancing. We grabbed all of the coats and threw them into the centre of the cloakroom and turned off the light-switch (which turned off all the lights in the ballroom as well). Then we "scurried" back down the pipe which was next to the fire escape stairs, and slid down the rope to the street. (We were too "light" to make the stairs go down), and had a good laugh about it.

It was such a good "prank" that we decided that we would do it again. So, several days later, we were back up in the cloak-room. Ray and I again "dumped" the coats on the floor, and turned off the light. We heard someone yell, "They are in there again; get 'em"! Let me tell you, we were out of there so fast! However, as I was hurrying down the rope to the street, I got my foot cut on the rope hook that was holding the awning. My foot was bleeding so bad, that when I got home my shoe was full of blood and my mother had to bandage it (you didn't go to the doctor in those days, unless it was very serious, as it was too expensive).

One summer, I guess I was around the age of ten or eleven years old, some friends and I were playing down by Juneau Park and we decided that we would all go swimming. We had a great time until it was time to head home and I remembered that I hadn't brought a towel with me; so I figured that I would just "roll" in the grass and that way I could dry off a little bit. I did and we headed home. Later that evening, I "broke out" in small blisters all over my body; I had rolled in some poison ivy! My mother bathed me in a "yellow" soap, which was the recommended "cure" for poison ivy, it didn't work, it just made it worse and I guess I almost died from it.

Even today my skin is so sensitive to it, that it actually "tingles" whenever I am near poison ivy. I also found out, that you should use alcohol to wash your skin if you come in contact with it, as anything made with oil, such as soap, just spreads the blisters.

After my father died and around the time I was twelve years old, I got a job working at the Red Cross, where I cleaned offices for twenty-five cents per hour after school and on Saturdays.

I worked four hours every day during the week from five o'clock p.m. until nine o'clock p.m. and I worked from eight a.m. to twelve o'clock noon on Saturdays. That was the day I cut the grass on the Red Cross property which was about four hundred feet wide and four hundred feet long. To do this I used a hand push-type lawn mower which was a very hard job if the grass was allowed to get too high.

I attended a Catholic Parochial school which started at seven- thirty in the morning, because you attended mass at that time, and then school would start at eight. You had one hour off for lunch, so I would run home, eat and run back to school; (lunch was from twelve noon to one o'clock p.m.). Then I would run home when school was over for the day at four o'clock, get my bike and ride it to and from work twice a day. The only day I didn't work was on Sunday when I would do my school work after church. I guess it was a good thing that I was a good student and smart enough so I could do this and still get good grades.

When I went to ask for a job, they asked if I was eighteen years old, I said I was and I got the job. But I think the real reason I got the job, was that the U.S. was involved in WWII at that time and there was no one else available.

When I had time off, I would bicycle up to Cedarburg, Wisconsin (about 20 miles from Milwaukee) to visit Mr. Mertons and his sister who were friends of my parents. One time during the summer, when I was bicycling to Cedarburg to see them, I spotted a Piper Cub airplane landing at old Brown Deer Airport (it is no longer there) and was totally fascinated by it, so much so, that I would bicycle out there after my work at the Red Cross on Saturday afternoons and would do odd jobs around the airport such as gassing planes, cleaning windshields, checking oil and moving planes into hangars in exchange for receiving flying lessons.

 One of the pilots there gave me flying lessons, and he soloed me as he thought I had a student pilot's license. When I finally did go to get my student pilot's license, I had two hundred hours of solo flying time logged into my book. The pilot who taught me to fly was quite surprised to find out I not only did not have a student pilot's license, but I wasn't yet sixteen. When I actually turned sixteen, I got my student pilot's license and several months later I applied and received my private pilot's license. This was truly the start of my love affair with flying.

Successfully designed as a simple, rugged and easy-to-fly light aeroplane for private owners, the Cub was cheap and could be flown from small airfields. This with a low landing speed of only 30 m.p.h. (50 km.p.h.) spelt instant success and over 760 had been sold by the end of 1936. Different engines were fitted to the later, widely exported models, which helped America gain her present lead in light aircraft.

PIPER CUB 1935

BUILT BY
Taylor Aircraft, Pennsylvania
DIMENSIONS
Length
 22.5 ft. (6.86 m.)
Wing span
 35.1 ft. (10.7 m.)
Weight empty
 560 lb. (254 kg.)
MAX. SPEED
87 m.p.h. (140 km.p.h.)
CEILING
12,000 ft. (3,650 km.) fully loaded
RANGE
210 miles (340 km.)
ENGINE
One 40 h.p. Continental A.404

Figure 11: I saw this "little beauty" and it was "love at first sight".

 As I mentioned previously, Ray Stuiber was my very best friend, and we did a lot of things together. I have to tell you about the time during the summer that we were both twelve. Well, Ray, I, my brother Carl and Ray's brother Jack went down to Juneau Park beach in Milwaukee, Wisconsin on Lake Michigan, to catch some crayfish for our dinners. It was very hot that day and we decided to take a "dip" in Lake Michigan instead to cool off. Well, I wanted to beat everyone to the beach and be the first one into the water.

There was a large lagoon, about one-half mile long and two hundred feet wide, which usually had a lot of ducks swimming on it; between me and the beach, so to save myself some time I figured I could make a shallow dive and be at the beach before anyone else. I knew the lagoon was shallow so I made a very shallow dive, almost a "belly-flop" into the water. What I didn't "know", was that the lagoon was only a couple of inches deep and full of rusty sharp metal (which I didn't see because the water was too dark). Anyway, I got cut up pretty bad, all the way from my chest down to the tops of my thighs.

I threw my towel over me, as I was very embarrassed, and Ray helped me back to the Red Cross Building where I worked, which was behind us and up an eight hundred foot very steep hill. As I walked, my runners left bloody foot-prints behind with each step. When we got to the Red Cross, Ray grabbed a big bottle of iodine, I took off my towel, which by this time was covered in blood, and Ray poured that whole bottle of iodine all over the front of me. Boy, did that stuff sting!!!

Another time, Ray and I found this artificial leg in an empty refrigerator at the Red Cross, and we both thought that it would be a funny joke if we put the leg on the floor and tipped the fridge over on it, to make it look as though someone was trapped underneath. So we both yelled as loudly as we could and carefully tipped the fridge over and then let it go "thump". Ray started screaming and yelling and then we just waited for someone to come and see what all the noise was about. Pretty soon a nurse came running in and saw the leg sticking out from under the fridge and started calling for help. Well we could see that now things were starting to get a little out of hand, so we stepped- up and confessed what we had done and that we had only meant it for a practical joke. Wow, was she ever mad at us!! She told us it really wasn't funny and someone really could have gotten hurt.

We didn't think it was quite so funny anymore.

Chapter Four

So Much to Do, So Much to Learn

The year is now 1944, and WWII is still going on. I was the grand old age of about fifteen years old, when I purchased a 1936 Pontiac car for the grand sum of three hundred dollars. It was a nice car but it needed some work. So at night after school, I would go to a Vocational School where they taught me, both the theory and principals of auto mechanics.

I was also lucky, as just a few doors down from where I lived, an old guy who owned a service station saw that I was interested in auto mechanics and decided to take me "under his wing". He taught me how to grind the valves, replace piston rings, fit the bearings and also supervised the rebuilding of the engine for my car, until I had it running perfectly. I now had some better "wheels", instead of just my bike. All I had to do was wait until I was sixteen and then I could get my driver's license. Of course not having a license did not mean that I couldn't drive, I just had to make sure that I made all of the stops perfect, did not speed or go to slow. My theory was to just obey all of the traffic laws and I would be alright !

Sometime around this time, oh I was about fifteen or possibly just sixteen; I got a job as the manager of the Perelese Office Building across the street from City Hall and the Pabst Theatre in Milwaukee, where we were able to move into one of the smaller office units to live. I ran the elevator before and after school, cleaned the halls, bathrooms and did general maintenance. While I was at school, my mother ran the elevator. I got the job from a doctor who owned the building and needed someone during WWII, as there were not a lot of people around available to work. He asked me if I was eighteen (you were supposed to be eighteen to hold a job), but I was big for my age so I have to say that I lied, and said,

" Yes". But I needed the money to help support my mother and brother so what else could I do? I had taken on the position of "Head" of my

22

family.

In school I was a pretty good student, nothing really spectacular like straight A's but good, especially if the subject interested me. Of course I would read any book I got my hands on, if it was something I was truly interested in, such as auto mechanics, carpentry, photography, flying and so forth.

While I was in high school, I did a little boxing, but after seeing the condition of some of the professional boxers, and how slurred their speech was in those days, I decided it really wasn't for me. I have to say that the few times I got hit in the head or jaw; I could actually feel my brain "shake". I guess you could say, I saw "stars".

I tried out for gymnastics while I was in high school and was good enough that I was put on the gymnastic team. I really enjoyed this as I was quite athletic. My specialty was the giant rings and rope climbing without using my legs, (I guess all that practice I had climbing up the rope in St. John's Cathedral bell tower with Ray, really did pay off and came in handy after all). I would have liked to pursue this a little bit more while I was in school, but my jobs kept me from being able to do so.

Figure 12: St John's Cathedral. Ray and I climbed to the bell tower of this beautiful building.

Like I said, I had a lot of different interests, just about anything that captured my imagination I would try. I would first read all that I could on the subject until I understood it perfectly, then I would practice working at doing it until I had it perfected it to my liking. One of these was photography that "peaked" my interest. The first thing I did when I got interested in something, as I said before, was to read about it.

Which meant that a trip to the library was the next step to learning all I could about cameras, both the taking and developing of pictures. After I had read up on the subject and thoroughly understood all that I had read, I purchased an old "box" style camera and started to take pictures. I was good enough at this that I became the family "picture taker" and I took pictures of everything I saw. Of course at time, you must remember that all of the pictures were in black and white, not like today which are in color.

I guess that my talent with the camera came in handy when I was later in business and had to make pictures for our brochures and advertising.

I even tried my hand at developing my own pictures, but it was just too costly an operation to do at that time, because of all the chemicals and solutions you had to buy to develop the pictures.

Another thing that "peaked" my interest was making furniture, and I took a wood working class in school to learn more about it. There we were taught the skills needed to make furniture. Later on, I used these same skills to make all the beds, chairs, table and cabinets that we had in our cabin on Lone Stone Lake at Three Lakes, Wisconsin. One problem I developed from learning to do wood work, is that I can tell when furniture is of good quality or cheaply made.

Figure 15: With a "goose" from Horicon Marsh north of Milwaukee, Wisconsin.

I was also quite an avid hunter, during the duck and goose hunting season, I would take my brother Carl and go to Horicon Marsh, which is sixty miles North West of Milwaukee, Wisconsin.

We were allowed to hunt our limit of water fowl (ducks and geese) but we could also shoot up to twenty five Mud Hens (a type of duck) a piece. We would get our limit and then we would give the Mud Hens to a Game Warden we knew, who knew how to cook the Mud Hens, we kept the ducks and geese, they made for very good eating.

Figure 18: Fly-fishing in northern Wisconsin near our cabin on Lone Stone Lake.

Figure 14: Me with a good sized "Musky" in front of my 1936 Pontiac car in northern Wisconsin.

Figures 19 & 20: My mother and also her standing in front of my Pontiac on our trip to California . when I was seventeen.

During the summer I was seventeen, I took my brother Carl and our mother on a vacation out to California. At the time the best road to travel to go to California, was old Route 66. One funny thing that happened (although it wasn't funny at the time) was at one of our gas stops when we were putting gas in the car. My mother, who was sitting in the back, got out to use the gas station washroom and didn't tell us nor did we see her leave the car. After we finished gassing the car, we hopped in, closed the doors and started driving. About a half an hour or forty-five minutes later when our mother had not answered one of our questions, we discovered that she was "missing", you know, Not There! Carl and I were asking each other, where was Ma ? What happened to her and did you see her leave? We had no idea where she was because we did not know when she had gotten out of the car. So we turned around and started searching for her at each place we passed. We finally found her at the service station where we had gassed the car, quietly and patiently waiting for us to discover her missing and come back and get her. She didn't say a single word to either of us !!!

Our vacation trip to California lasted around two weeks and we had a chance to cover a lot of ground and saw a lot of interesting things.

Well we ended up only living at the Perelese Office Building for about a year, when my half-brother Max, convinced me that, I could make more money working with him washing high-rise office windows. So we left the Perelese and moved into a house on North Water Street where Max and his wife were living at the time, (I was supporting my mother so that my brother Carl could remain in school).

We arrived at the house, sixteen forty North Water Street to find it was a three storey building with Max, his wife Juanita (we called her Jane) and three small children living in the first floor apartment which had a heaved wooden floor and quite badly in need of repair. My mother, my bother Carl and I moved into the apartment on the second floor.

After we were there awhile, my interest turned to how to correct the problem of Max's apartment. So back to the library I went to find the information I would need. I also talked to different building contractors about the problem. Back then the building contractors came up with a new solution, it was to use a mixture of asbestos with a type of hardening liquid which could be purchased and delivered by a concrete hauling truck. So I talked my brother Carl into helping me rip out the whole first floor and ordered the "stuff". I had it delivered and poured into a six inch thick asbestos floor which was forty by thirty feet. On top of this, I installed copper tubing back and forth three or four feet apart and covered it with four inches of concrete. The tubing was then connected to a hot water boiler so there was radiant (warm) heat in the concrete, making the floors and the entire room warm. I found that this worked extremely well and that all of my reading and talking to people in the industry really did pay off, and there were now nice warm floors in the apartment.

I am going to take a moment now and tell you of an interesting happening, which was right next door to where we were living on North Water Street. There was a tavern next door that was owned by this man we knew by the name of Nick Lupo. We got along with him real well, in fact the house we were living in was owned by him and we were renting. Nick offered to let us buy the house, and we could pay him for it in our monthly rental payments with no down payment required. Well one day we noticed a lot of large black limousines and big Cadillacs with the license plates from out of state, (particularly from Illinois). We did not think too much about it until all of a sudden, we spotted a lot of police cars parked out on the street, and the police, taking pictures of the license plates on the cars. That was when we realized that there was a "Mob" meeting going on next door. The papers the next day, signified that Mr. Nick Lupo was a "Godfather" in the Mafia. Wow, that was something to know !

While I was still going to high school, I also kept working towards getting my commercial pilot's license on weekends (I needed 200 hours to get the commercial license, which I got by the way), when I was around eighteen or nineteen years old. Also during this time I worked off and on for my half-brother Max washing office windows.

One incident that sticks out in my mind while I was working for Max, was the time the belt I was wearing, while washing the windows let loose because the bolt-heads were rusted. I had to quickly "grab" the other side of the belt to keep myself from falling.

Let me explain what I am talking about. There were large bolts on each side of the window that you washed and this is what you fastened your belt to. The belt I wore was a wide heavy leather belt with heavy canvas straps on each side of the belt. You would attach these straps to the bolts on the side of the window. These windows were approximately three feet wide and seven feet tall office windows that we washed, and the buildings could be from six to twenty stories high. So you can understand how dangerous this could be when a bolt came loose or came out completely. I only did this for about one year.

I also painted houses while I was going to school and during the summer, I even spray-painted the inside of a slaughter house near where we lived. I was using lead-based paint at that time and became very sick with Yellow Jaundice, (this is when the skin and eyes become yellow due to excess bile in the blood) I was very sick, feverish and head-achy, but I kept right on working. This condition lasted for around two or more weeks.

Hey, you do what you have to do.

Chapter Five

Ready to Taxi

When I finished high school, I took a job working at the Schlitz Brewing Company, where I worked third shift (this is midnight to eight in the morning) parking semi-trailer trucks as well as driving a Hough tractor to move strings of railroad boxcars in and out of Schlitz Brewing docks.

I'm going to tell you what a Hough Tractor was and how it was used. The Hough tractor had tires seven feet high, the bumper was ten feet wide, four feet high and it was about a foot thick, with steel plates on each side and solid hard rubber in between. The reason for this was, so you could move eight or ten boxcars at a time. These "cars" were lined up in a railroad yard on tracks and they had to be moved inside of the brewery railroad loading docks. To do this you would hook a chain twenty feet long with links about four inches wide to the coupling, release the boxcar air-brakes and move up to ten boxcars at a time by "ramming" the hitch as hard as you could to get the cars moving. Once the cars were moving at a couple of miles per hour, you would slowly "back off" so as not to break the chain, the moving boxcars would keep on moving ahead and would then pull the tractor along with the cars. When you were ready to "spot them", you would "slowly- brake" them until you were signaled to stop.

Also during the winter, when I finished working at Schlitz Brewery at eight o'clock in the morning, I would hurry over to the Milwaukee School of Engineering, where I attended school three days a week, from nine o'clock in the morning until twelve o'clock noon. Studying electrical engineering (my afternoons were off) and I would go out to Brown Deer Airport and fly or I'd work with my brother Max, washing windows. I would get home just before five-thirty at night have something to eat go to bed for about five hours, get up and go to work again at Schlitz.

Figure 21: Schlitz Brewery with train cars
that I used to park with a Hough tractor.

Figure 22: This is a picture of a Hough Tractor similar
to the one I used to drive. The one I drove had tires
six feet high and was used to move the train cars.

In the summer, my routine was similar, except I didn't go to school. Around this time I became interested in building houses. Again I did my research by reading everything I could find on building and construction. Paul Oldenburg, a pilot I knew at Brown Deer Airport, (in fact I had gassed his plane and cleaned his windows many times), was a building contractor. He had three lots that already had foundations installed just waiting for the houses to be built. He agreed to "take me under his wing" and show me how to build a floor and put walls up for a house. He watched and supervised me for awhile and then left me on my own, only coming back later to check on my work. He told me I was doing a good job and to keep it up and left. I finished putting in the floor and walls.

He later offered to give me a lot which had a foundation already on it, in exchange for "roughing in" two buildings that he was working on. I had never done this "roughing in" before, but I had done a lot of reading on the subject so I felt I could do it.

Paul then had the plumbing and wiring put in and I came back and did the insulation and drywall. This was the start of my house building.

On weekends and the days I wasn't working, I was flying, and when I finally got my commercial pilot's license, I started flying charters for Bob Huggins out of Brown Deer Airport. When I started getting more charters, I quit my job at Schlitz Brewery and the Milwaukee School of Engineering to fly full time.

While I was doing charters I met this young pilot who told me about flying for Walt Disney, (who was at that time buying up land around Orlando, Florida, by having independent agencies do the buying for him, but not using his name). That way the cost of the property would not be inflated. This same young pilot told me about flying in South America with Walt Disney and finding diamonds and other precious stones in the rivers down there, especially in the Orinoco River in Venezuela, he said you could actually "pick them up out of the water".

Figures 26 & 27: These are two of the airplanes I flew charters with for Bob Huggins at Old Brown Deer Airport. A Cessna 180 and a Beech Bonanza

After talking to this guy for a while, I figured that this could be a great experience. So I talked my brother Carl, into going with me. I was flying a four passenger all metal Stinson Station Wagon with a Met-Co-Aire Conversion airplane down to Venezuela to take a look for ourselves. On our way to South America, we stopped over in San Jose, Costa Rica. There I met a young man who was having trouble landing his plane and taking-off. I told him I would be happy to show him the proper way to take-off and land his Cessna 195 airplane. I did this, and he thanked me for my help and asked if I would like a job flying for him, being his private pilot. He said, I would be well paid and could even have my own private house. But he needed someone to fly him, so he could check on the progress of the road that was being built. (This was the Pan-American Highway) I felt that I had to turn him down, as I really wanted to go down to Venezuela and maybe find some of those "gem stones" that I had been told about, also, I had my brother Carl along with me.

Later on, I found out that I had turned down a job from the President of Colombia's son. Boy, can you imagine what things could have been like if I had taken the job? Oh well, I guess one can always say that "hind-sight" is better than "foresight". Anyway, we didn't find any gems, but we saw a lot of Piranhas in the water and decided it was not worth the problems we could have with those small flesh-eating fish.

However, while I was down there, I was approached by several men who were looking to get some of the U.S. military WWII surplus aircraft. There were quite a few just sitting around for sale after WWII and very cheap. For instance, I bought a Stearman airplane with a spare engine for about four hundred dollars and even a P-51 fighter with a full tank of gas, for about six hundred. I loved flying the P-51 but the cost of the fuel used to fly it, cost a couple of week's wages, so I had to sell it. Anyway, back to the surplus WWII airplanes. When I talked to the men, I got their names and how to get in contact with them, and said that I would take a look around and see what I could find. I was told that I would be paid a good commission and have all of my expenses paid if I was able to get some aircraft. And that was the start of my ferrying aircraft to South

America.

Back then there was no internet, and the telephone service between the U.S. and South America was not that good, so you would have to use telegrams, which took quite awhile to communicate back and forth with prospective airplane buyers. I guess all in total, I sold about seven airplanes within the year and a half that I was doing it.

In June of 1948, I joined the Wisconsin National Guards, where I served one day a week, every other weekend, and two to three weeks every summer. During the time I was in the Guards, I also learned to fly an L-19 surveillance plane and even got checked-out in an F-88 fighter jet down in Alabama.

Sometime around late 1949 or 1950, I got a job flying for Clintonville Airways as their chief pilot, the pay was not that good and the pay was always late in coming, so I only stayed with them for about three months when I quit. I also felt that the Clintonville Airways was kind of a "Mickey Mouse" operation. Who would have guessed at that time that they would become North Central Airlines and eventually Republic Airlines?

When I was in my early twenties, my brother Carl and our half-brother Max took a canoe trip up north of Ely, Minnesota in the Quatico Provincial Park (there were virtually no tourists going into there at that time). We took several weeks planning this trip, right down to the last detail. We brought dried food, coffee, matches soaked in wax so they couldn't get wet, flour, sugar, all of our equipment, mosquito spray along with hats that had mosquito nets on them. We even had a big piece of bacon double smoked and hung for a couple of weeks so that all of the fat would be out of it so it would keep. We planned to live- off the land the rest of the time. We were gone for about three weeks. When we returned home, the pair of hiking boots that I had purchased new for the trip were almost worn out. I can tell you we lost weight, although I do not remember how much, but, Boy, were we in good shape !!!

Also, after we got back home, we found out that the U.S. was at war with Korea, but it took me a long time to really find out exactly what happened to get the U.S. into a war again.

Figure 28: This is a picture of a WWII airplane. It is a P-51 fighter plane. You were able to buy them quite cheap after the war. I loved this plane but the fuel was very costly so I sold it.

Figure 29 & 30: I joined the National Guards in June of 1948 and attained the rank of Sergeant in the military police.

Back in the Guards, I found out that anyone who had a pilot's license was "practically guaranteed" on being "shipped" over to Korea. Since I really did not want to go overseas, I immediately joined the M.P. (Military Police) Company, where I served until I was honorably discharged in May of 1956.

During this time, my company was put on "alert" several times and we were even told to sell everything and get prepared to leave; then we would be told to "stand down," and we didn't leave. After doing this several times and even selling my cars, I decided that the next time we were put on "alert"; I was going to hang-on to my car. We never did go overseas or get into the "conflict".

While in the National Guards, I achieved the rank of Sergeant; and also won my "Sharp-Shooter's" badge. I guess all that hunting I did, really paid off big time!

Most of my duties were to keep a watch on the camp and to go into town for "town patrol" when the "men" were on town-leave. Usually when the men were on "town-leave", the M.P.'s would go into town and go to the police station where we had a desk for our use. If a call came in both the police and the M.P.'s would go out and investigate. The M.P's took care of military persons and the police took care of the civilians.

After the bars closed, the M.P's would look for any military men still wandering around or passed-out on the street. We would also check on the movie theatres when they closed, as sometimes the M.P.'s would find soldiers who had fallen asleep in different areas of the theatre.

I remember one very embarrassing moment I had while on "town patrol" checking out an empty movie theatre. I was completely dressed in my uniform, which first of all has a lot of parts that you have to wear. Well anyway, I had to use the washroom very badly, I quickly rushed into the nearest washroom and hurried into a stall, There I proceeded to get undressed as quickly as I could, this included not only taking down my trousers, unfastening my belt, but also taking off my pistol belt with my

37

pistol, my lanyard and my night stick, which took a lot of doing in such a small confined space. Well, as "luck" would have it, I heard someone else come in the washroom and enter the stall next to mine. I happened to look down towards the floor and spotted a skirt on the floor next to me, and I immediately realized my mistake, I had entered the WOMEN's Washroom and not the MEN's in the semi-dark. Can we talk about a complete panic? I got dressed faster than I ever had before and got the "heck out of Dodge".

Figure 24: This is me carrying the canoe on our trip to Quatico Provincial Park. I am in my early 20's with my brothers, Max and Carl.

Figure 31: Max and Carl are carrying the packs on our canoe trip.

If we (the M.P.'s) got a report of any bar fights or any kind of a disturbance in a public place, we were trained to look for the highest ranking officer, approach him only and inform him, that if he did not get his men under control, that he would be the first to be arrested for not having control of the men under his command.

One time I was chasing this General who was always getting drunk and causing problems, I saw him take off down a road that I was not familiar with in a Jeep, so I grabbed my Harley motorcycle and took off after him. We were going at a very high rate of speed, I did not know exactly where we were going, but I guess he did, as he lead me down a road where a six foot gap across the road was filled with sand . When the front wheel hit the sand, The Harley and I flew end over end several times and after I landed, I was sure that every bone in my body had been broken! The Harley was so damaged that it could not be ridden, so I radioed for help to come get me. After I got back, I told the Platoon Commander, that that would be the last time; I would get on a motorcycle.

And THAT WAS THE LAST TIME, I was ever one again!

Figure 25: A picture of "Canoe Country Out-fitters" in Ely, Minnesota just before we went on our canoe trip.

Chapter Six

I've Got My Wings Now Let Me Ferry

During the time I was serving in the National Guards, I ferried many airplanes to South America in the year and a half I was doing it. There was pretty good money to be made in it and I had many exciting and interesting adventures along the way. For instance, I flew my Stinson aircraft through a valley in Venezuela to see the famous Angel Falls, the tallest waterfall in the world and got some very spectacular pictures of the falls themselves. I have to say, that this was some Pretty Scary flying now that I look back on it, but at the time it was just very exciting!

I ferried many different airplanes to many different places in South America, some of these places were: Cuidad, Bolivar, Caracas, Venezuela, Bogota, Columbia and San Jose, Costa Rica just to name a few.

Figures 32, 33, & 34: These are three of the airplanes that I ferried to South America, a Gull Wing Stinson, a Norseman and a Twin Beech. There were several others I have not included.

I'm going to take a few minutes and explain how I went about ferrying airplanes to South America. As I told you before, all communications were done by telegrams back and forth between me and the prospective airplane buyers. After finding the requested aircraft, the first thing I would do was check out the airplane for any mechanical problems or any items that looked like they might break down on the aircraft.

40

The next thing I did was to figure out how much fuel I would need so that I would only have to make two stops for gas after leaving the U.S. border. When the fuel consumption was figured out, I had Carl help me build wooden racks to hold portable ferry tanks which would hold the extra fuel needed. The ferry tanks we used were surplus military fuel tanks which we would stack in the wooden frames in the rear of the aircraft, as many as we had room for.

Next I found that the best way to get the fuel into the aircraft fuel system, was to drill a hole in the aircraft gas cap and then to weld a tube to the hole and "run" a rubber line from the cap through an aircraft air ventilation opening, to the centre of the two front seats. Between the two front seats was a "selector valve" which was used to choose from one of the four to six ferry tanks I had with me.

I then connected this to an electric fuel pump as well as a backup hand operated fuel pump called a "wobble pump" that you used by moving the handle back and forth or "wobble" to put fuel into the main gas tanks of the airplane, in case the electric gas pump failed. This method enabled you to fly a longer distance and avoid making too many custom/immigration gas stops, as each stop would take up to a minimum of three hours. Another time, I asked Carl to go with me to South America to deliver an airplane. I did all the flying, and my brother Carl would have to do the "wobbling" of the fuel if it became necessary.

When the aircraft fuel tank (usually the right wing tank) got to the half full condition, the fuel would be pumped into the aircraft tank from a ferry tank until the airplane tank was almost full again.

The non-stop flight path I would use if I was flying a single engine airplane, was from Milwaukee, Wisconsin to Brownsville, Texas on the southern U.S. border; this was the time that if there were any problems, they could be found and fixed before flying over some very desolate barren areas.

I would file an International Flight Plan from Brownsville, Texas to Tapachula, Mexico on the Nicaraguan border. The next day, I would file a flight plan to San Jose, Costa Rica, and then one to Panama City, Panama where I would fly along the West Central American coast line of South America to Caracas, Venezuela and from there on to several various deli-

41

very points.

Figure 35: One of my first stops ferrying airplanes down to South America, Tapachula, Mexico

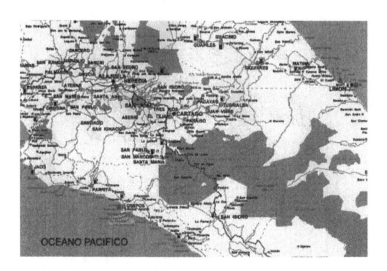

Figure 36: Second stop, San Jose, Costa Rica

If I was delivering a twin engine aircraft, I would fly a different route. This one would be from Milwaukee, Wisconsin to Key West, Florida and then on down past the Caribbean Islands so that I could stay near airports in case I had any problems.

During the 1950's, there were no roads to Tapachula, Mexico, the airport was very rough and primitive. In fact, every one hundred feet, they had a four foot wide ditch filled with porous gravel lying across the runway.(I guess this was so the tropical rain could drain off the runway).

Fuel was available from fifty gallon gas drums; which had to be pumped out with a hand-pump, as I said, very primitive. There were apparently no private aircraft or very few ever landed there. The few tourists that did come to Mexico at that time drove by car to the central region of Mexico and very few private aircraft used any of the Mexican airports.

The Mexican customs and airport personnel were so corrupt, that it would take a "book" to tell you all of the things they did to try and extort money from the rare travelers at that time. Well after taking off the next day at dawn for the next "leg" of the flight down to San Jose, Costa Rica , we were about three hours into the flight and were flying along the Pacific Ocean coast line, the aircraft engine started to "run rough ". Then about thirty minutes later, the engine slowly started to lose power. I began looking along the coast for a beach that would be long enough to land the airplane on, but the area we were flying over only had very large rock cliffs along the shore as far as we could see.

I tried the engine primer pump and slowly pumped it, but to no avail, it only seemed to cause the engine to "run rougher" and the aircraft engine was still slowly losing more power; in fact by this time, we had lost about four hundred RPM of our power. We were still holding our altitude, but with a much slower flying speed, the RPM kept slowing down which also slowed down our airspeed to a point we were starting to very slowly also lose our altitude.

I then tried the throttle accelerator pump and found out, that if I would slowly push it in and pull it out half way, and then slowly push it back in, the engine would hold enough power to not lose any more altitude.

The decision had to be made of turning east over some very rough terrain towards San Jose or keep flying along the coast and try and find a sand beach. I decided that landing in rough terrain was better than trying to land on the bottom of the two hundred to eight hundred foot cliffs. Well we "limped" all the way to San Jose and there I made a perfect landing, but found that the runway surface was so hot that the landing gear

43

wheels were "throwing" melted black tar up to the underside of the wings. What a Mess that made !! Then as we were taxing to the terminal, we heard a "thump, thump, thump"; looking down at the main gear tires, it looked like a small bulge in one of the tires.

After parking the airplane, I discovered that the wheel rim or "bead" that holds the tire had a four inch break in it. I guess the heavy load we had taking off at the Tapachula Airport and the draining "ruts" running across the runway had caused the damage.

After dealing with customs and immigration, we found a super modern repair facility on the airport that did repairs on aircraft from all over Central and South America. By luck, a mechanic who spoke perfect English, and who befriended us, said that I should go to the Pan American Airline Terminal and talk to one of the captains there, as they flew every day to and from the U.S. I told a Pan Am captain my problem, gave him the aircraft make and wheel manufacturer and the tire size. You know, I still can't believe this, the next flight from the U.S. had a new wheel delivered for me, and when I asked how much I owed them, I was told, there was no charge, but to consider this a "goodwill" gesture from Pan American Airlines. I took the wheel and gave him our "thanks".

The day after I spoke with the English speaking mechanic who offered us coffee, and I commented, "that I had never tasted any coffee like this; it was so smooth and flavorable". He then told us, that the coffee bought in the U.S., Canada and most of the world was their number #3 grade of coffee, he said that a few countries would buy the number #2 grade, but only Germany and France bought the number #1 grade of premium coffee, and this was their number #1 grade of coffee that we were drinking. I have to say, that that was the Best coffee I have ever had!!

I had brought along a few basic mechanic tools and I mentioned that I was going to "pull" off the carburetor and check it out. While I was taking the carburetor off, I found that the whole "bowl" was full of short and long strands of something that looked much smaller than a hair. I spoke to the mechanic about this and he informed me that I must have gassed the airplane from fuel drums.

When I inquired how he knew this was the reason for all of the fine micro-slivers I had found; he said, "the fuel drums had a coating inside so that they did not rust when they were partially empty". When the drums that weighted over three hundred pounds, were handled, even just rolling the drums, caused these small fine slivers to break off from the sides.

These drums were shipped to a crude ocean port near Tapachula, Mexico and then had to be hand loaded onto a donkey cart and taken to the air-port which was several miles from the ocean shipping pier. Also, the gas had to be "hand-pumped" and it was not filtered.

We were told, that when we fueled up the airplane at Tapachula, there must have only been a few gallons of aviation fuel left in the first drum; and when the next two drums had been rolled over so we could finish gassing our airplane, we had gotten the contaminates that were floating in suspension from the moving of the drums, in our gas tanks.

The mechanic asked me why I did not filter the fuel. I showed him the large funnel with the fine mesh in the bottom that I had with me and had been using. I was told that the funnel was totally useless. He then pro-ceeded to show me a "felt filter" which he said was the only thing to use as it would not allow any water or material no matter how small, to pass through. The funnel, even though it had a fine mesh, could not stop any of the slivers from passing through the mesh and into our gas tanks.

He told me to buy a "blank" felt hat from a hat manufacturer; so I im-mediately offered to pay him three times more for his "felt hat filter" than was the actual cost of it. That felt hat filter "broke the bank" at twelve dollars! I've had, and used that same felt "hat filter" for over sixty years and keep it in every airplane I have had, including my original metal funnel.

After learning this" trick ", I was even able to use fuel that other people would discard. When you use the "filter," you keep adding fuel until it slows down and then you pull it out of the funnel, turn it inside out and "beat " it on a clean object or even your wing strut. All of the dirt, water and grime come out.

It works so well, that on my seaplane charters, I would carry aviation fuel in my floats, (all floats have some water seepage), I could use a hand float pump and pump the fuel into a pail and then pour it into my felt hat filter. I have never had a problem, doing this in over, my sixty years of flying and I have probably filtered hundreds of gallons of "dirty" fuel.

Anyway, back to my story, I gave the mechanic my carburetor and he soaked it in a carburetor cleaning solution; I then checked all of the fuel valves, etc., and reassembled everything and was again able to get on our way.

But I had my first learning "curve" and I never had any real problems after that. In fact, I didn't even make much out of the entire episode, but upon thinking back, I have to say, that nothing really fazes a young kid, no matter what seems to happen.

The rest of the trip went smoothly, except for the usual corrupt customs and immigration officials, and I have to say that all of the time I spent in those countries, that not once did I ever meet an honest government employee.

The another thing you needed to know, was how to "deal" with the customs and immigration officials in these other countries, because back then all of the custom and immigration officials were " corrupt " and always willing to extort money from the unwary traveler, which there were very few of at that time. So you always made sure that you had ALL of your paper work along with you and then you played the "game" of "customs and immigration twenty questions," which would go something like this. You land, a Customs and Immigration official would come out to the plane and would first ask if the aircraft had been decontaminated; you would then show them the can of spray you had with you.

Then you were escorted to their office under military guard where he would ask for another paper he needed, you would look for that paper (you always knew you had it, but you had to pretend to look for it), he would always offer to "let it go" if you would pay him fifty dollars or so. Next you would "find" the paper he had asked for and hand it to him, he would look at it and hand it back.

Next he would ask for another paper and again you would go through the process of "looking" and him offering to let you get by without it if you would give him fifty dollars, of course you would again "find" it. This game would go on for a while, until he ran out of documents and things to ask for.

46

I always carried a copy of the flight plan with me, in case they said, they hadn't received it. I also had my passport, personal pilot licenses, immunization record, personal police report history, birth certificate, all aircraft documents, proof of aircraft purchaser and final destination And a spray can of insect decontaminate.

The next thing he would ask is how long I was planning on staying and he would imply that some military guard would watch my plane over night to keep it from being vandalized or fuel stolen. It was always implied that he would see that it was taken care of for a fee. I would tell him "good", and that I was planning on leaving at about nine or ten o'clock in the morning. I would then gas the plane that night and leave at dawn the next morning, and no guards were ever around.

Another time, when Carl joined me to ferry a plane to South America, we stopped in Costa Rica during their Mardi Gras, what a sight! Parades, music, dancing, everything was really exciting and colorful.

While we were there, I became acquainted with a man who was flying his Stinson airplane out to the San Blas Islands, off the coast of Panama to trade with the local native population. He told us that if we ever landed on the San Blas Islands and had to overnight, that we should make sure we stayed in our airplane and not try to camp out, as the natives were still quite primitive and might try to kill us.

But he said that if we wanted to follow him over there in our airplane just to have a "peek" we could see what it was like, he would not mind. So we followed him over there and watched him trade cheap cooking pots, mirrors and other trinkets for jaguar and alligator skins which he then sold for a lot of money. As we flew over the San Blas Islands, we also experienced the natives throwing spears at us, especially as we flew over Columbia.

We were told that we should always fly over the coast on the way to Caracas, Venezuela instead of flying over land, because, if we had to make an emergency landing, we could land on a beach. Where if we were forced to make a landing in the interior, there was a one-hundred percent chance of being killed by the natives at that time.

Actually, during the time I was flying airplanes to South America, there was a report in the news of five missionaries disappearing in that area when they were trying to make contact with the natives in Columbia. They were never heard of again. The airplane was found undamaged in a grass field, but the five missionaries or their remains were never found.

Another time when I landed for the first fuel, customs and immigration stop, it was in Tapachula, Mexico a small isolated community with no roads entering or leaving, which is on the Mexico/Nicaraguan border. I and Carl (who was with me on this trip) stayed overnight in the "best " hotel in town, actually, it was the ONLY hotel the town had to offer; you must remember at that time things were still a little "primitive", as there were very few and far between tourists traveling, not like it is today with all these different destinations and fancy hotels to stay in. Anyway our room overlooked the street, but it had neither screens nor glass on the windows, only shutters, which are made of wood and are a little like doors with "angled slats of wood for ventilation" attached to the windows and you can open them up. Our window was low enough that the passersby could look into our room. The shower they had was very unique. First of all it was outside the back door and had a curtain surrounding it for privacy. You stood upon a wooden palette and the water was held in a fifty gallon drum set up on a tripod and heated by the sun. You turned on a "sprinkler" type knob and there was your shower. A little primitive, but it worked!

Also in the morning, little donkeys could be heard clip-clopping past our room on the cobbled street below, and all of the "slops" and "chamber pots" would be emptied into the street as well.

One day while we were still in Tapachula, we decided to walk the one block to the plaza, when we got there we noticed that everyone seemed to be chewing something and were acting a little "stoned ". They would all chew this "stuff" and spit on the ground like someone chewing "snuff, " you know, like Copenhagen? Well, we found out that they were all chewing "Beetle Nut," a berry like thing that was highly narcotic. Well, that certainly explained the "stoned" look!

That night, shortly after we had turned out the light and were preparing to go to sleep, I heard a kind of "rustling scratching " noise, so I reached over and touched Carl (you see, we had worked out a plan, whereby if anyone would come into our room we would be prepared for them), so

Carl, grabbed the pistol and I grabbed the flashlight, jumped out of bed and turned on the flashlight. As my feet hit the floor, I felt and heard a "crunching" sound beneath my bare feet. When Carl turned on the overhead light, we saw the box which contained our pilot biscuits literally moving across the floor which was now full of large cockroaches When we told the owners (a redheaded woman from Vancouver who had married a man from down there), about the cockroaches, we were told that we should not worry too much about them, as the 'roaches were a sign that the room was clean and free of bedbugs because the cockroaches eat the bed bugs. Hey, great to know, thank you very much for the info!!

Another time when I was delivering an aircraft, and after Custom and Immigration had completely checked out both the airplane and me, I arrived back at the aircraft the next day to find large Government seals over each door, stating "DO NOT REMOVE", Venezuela Government Customs." I wondered, what in the heck was going on? Both I and the aircraft had been cleared by Customs and Immigration. So I walked over to the Government office on the airport and was told upon entering, that I was to be escorted by car to a Government office in downtown Caracas.

When we arrived I met an older gentleman who spoke English and Spanish. He told me, he was an American, and then informed me that the President of Venezuela wanted to ask me some questions. The gentleman and I talked a little about airplanes and then I was seated in a chair next to a small desk facing the Venezuelan President who was sitting at a large desk. The gentleman, acting as interpreter, sat in a chair beside me.

The President asked at least six to ten questions through the interpreter in Spanish, I replied in English back to the interpreter. After I had been asked and answered questions which I started to think were sounding kind of foolish, I said to the interpreter, "what kind of stupid "blankety, blank, blank, blank "questions are these"?

The interpreter, kicked me in the shin and whispered, "be careful, he speaks perfect English", Whoops! But I guess my answers or maybe my "language "? Pacified the Venezuelan President as I was told that the seals would be removed from the aircraft and I could be on my way. The interpreter walked me out of the office, shook my hand and said, "I'm Jimmie Angel by the way. "

49

Later, I realized, that the interpreter was the pilot who had discovered the famous Angel Falls in Venezuela, which are in fact named after him, and is the highest waterfall in the world. WOW !!!

Angel Falls in Venezuela.

On another of my trips ferrying airplanes to South America, I was invited by my customers to go out to dinner and "party" with them to celebrate the delivery of the aircraft. Hey, I was young (in my early twenties), so I said, "okay, let's go"!!

We went to one of the best night clubs in Caracas (where only the wealthy people, the politicians and the Top Military were welcome). After enjoying a great dinner, we partied for about four hours or maybe more (there were around three hundred people in the place at this time), when all of a sudden I heard a loud gunshot go off about sixty feet from our table. I looked up and saw a large group of people standing in a circle. I asked my companions what had happened? I was told, "a high ranking Military officer had shot a man who had verbally insulted him". When I asked if the police had been called, I was told, "NO, that things like this happened quite often and not to get involved." So I did what everyone else I was with was doing, and remained in my seat and kept my mouth

Membership Options

Choose the right card.

Executive Membership

With our highest level of membership, business members and individuals alike earn a 2% Reward on most of their Costco purchases* - up to $750 a year.
An Executive Membership is $110 per year (plus applicable taxes) and includes a FREE Spouse† card.

Gold Star Membership

Purchase high-quality, name brand products and services for personal use.
A Gold Star Membership is $55 per year (plus applicable taxes) and includes a FREE Spouse† card.

Business Membership

Available to business owners and managers, a Business Membership allows you to purchase products and services for business, personal and resale** use.
A Business Membership is $55 per year (plus applicable taxes) and includes a FREE Spouse† card.

For more information about Costco, drop by a warehouse, call 1-800-463-3783 or visit **Costco.ca**.

shut.

As the reason I was ferrying airplanes to South America in the first place was to make enough money so I could start my own flying business, I took a job as a "bush pilot " flying for U.S. Steel, actually for Borgia Aviation which had a contract with U.S. Steel, (Borgia Aviation was out of Cuidad, Bolivar) anyway, they were having trouble finding pilots willing or able to fly a Twin Beech aircraft in and out of a severely sloped mountain airstrip. Hey, I was young, foolish and fearless, why I was totally indestructible, so I took the job. When I think back on it now, I can't believe I actually did it!

After flying a few trips, I realized how dangerous it actually was and told them I was quitting, but they said, "If I would stay on and fly for them, they would double my wages". So I said, "Yes ", after all I was thinking about having my own flying business one day. I was flying about three to four trips per day bringing in supplies or men. There was always a "strong " military presence there and they watched you very carefully. They knew exactly how much fuel it would take to fly a round trip and they would not let you have any more fuel than that; but sometimes, depending on the weather, you needed extra fuel to make sure that you did not end up landing somewhere in the jungle due to not enough fuel on board.

After about a month with them, I again quit and again they said that they would double my wages, so I again agreed but this time 1 told them that I wanted to be paid in U.S. currency and in "cash" (I had been informed, that if you had money in the bank, you could not withdraw it and leave Venezuela and I DEFINITELY planned on leaving and returning to the U.S.).

I continued flying for them, for another three or four months and they doubled my wages several more times. After flying for them for about three months, I started to slowly withdraw my money from the bank. I had made an arrangement with Borgia Aviation that I would give them the Venezuelan currency and they would pay me back in U.S. dollars, this way I was able to get all of my money out of the bank.

While I was flying for them around three months, I slowly started to "sneak" about five gallons of fuel at a time to my own personal aircraft so

I could return to my home in the U.S. My airplane was a Stinson 165 Station Wagon with a Metco Air Conversion (this was an all metal aircraft, the original Stinsons were fabric). It took several months, but I finally had all the airplane tanks filled, plus several of my ferry tanks (they held about eighty-four extra gallons).

When I received my final cash payment from Borgia Aviation, I put all of my money into a money belt, (I had about eight thousand dollars at this time), when I went to the airport where my airplane was located, I noticed that there was no one around (it was about two or three o'clock on a Sunday morning) and decided that there was no time like the present to go home. So I loaded all of my personal gear into the airplane and "Took off without turning on my navigational lights and used my flashlight to see my instrument panel.

My plan was to "sneak" around Caracas and up the coast (which I did) and only flew about two to four hundred feet high so that I wouldn't be detected on radar (I was really worried about the Venezuelan Air Force because if they detected me, they would probably "shoot me down" as I had not filed an International Flight Plan).

So I flew the coast at no higher than four hundred feet all around Panama and Mexico, and stayed far away from any city or airport, like I said I wanted to stay away from any radar. Now I had been flying for about thirteen to fourteen hours and without sleep for almost forty-eight hours and I was almost to Brownsville, Texas when I started to get oil all over my wind shield making it hard to see out.

As I said before, I did not have an International Flight Plan so I did not dare to land in Mexico where I could end up losing my airplane and possibly even end up in jail, there was only one thing to do, and that was to continue flying on to Brownsville, Texas. Finally I was able to call the Brownsville Control Tower to ask for landing instructions. Before I could land, the tower asked why I had no International Flight Plan. Now you have to remember that first of all, that I had not had any sleep for more than forty-eight hours, I had been flying for at least fourteen hours AND my windshield was covered in oil and my visibility was VERY poor. In fact, to land I had to watch out the side windows to see and I had to "side-slip" the plane, so that I could land on the runway. I made a perfect landing, if I do say so myself!

Okay, as soon as I landed, I was told to go directly to the tower where I was to park the aircraft and not get out of the plane. I did as 1 was told and within minutes, several Police and Customs agents approached and started to interrogate me. I tried to answer their questions respectfully, but then one of the Customs agents started to get very abusive with me and started uttering threats.

Now I am not proud of this, but I lost it! I hauled-off and hit the Customs agent so hard in the head I thought I may have killed him.

I was immediately arrested, but I told the Immigration/Customs officers and Police, "that I would not talk to anyone else until I saw a U.S. Ambassador." It took a couple of hours, but the Ambassador arrived and I told him my story. He talked to the police and the Customs agent I had hit and then he told me to apologize and shake hands with the agent and I was then allowed to leave. I was almost HOME! "Good old U.S.A." !! I was finally back and my future now lay in front of me.

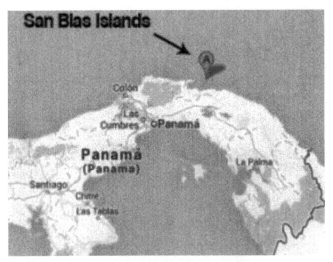

Figure 37: The San Blas Islands. The natives would throw spears at our airplane as we flew over the island.

Figure 38: Last stops, Caracas, Venezuela and Bogata, Columbia.

Chapter Seven

Open Water Here I Come

During the years that I was ferrying airplanes down to South America, I met an "underling" who worked for Fidel Castro the Dictator of Cuba. He approached me about using my plane to fly guns and ammunition over to Cuba; he said that there would "be no questions asked"! He told me, that I could make a lot of money doing this, but I felt that it would be very illegal as well as I would have felt like a "traitor" to my country to become a "gunrunner". So I said, "Thanks but no thanks", and I never saw nor heard from him again. I suppose they did find someone else to do it; there are always people who do not mind doing this kind of job but, it wasn't me.

In between the time, I wasn't on duty with the Wisconsin National Guards or ferrying planes to South America, I would fly up north to Three Lakes, Wisconsin, where I would land my Piper PA-12 on the airport, which was and still is a grass strip. There, I would spend time at a cabin we owned on Lone Stone Lake, or if the weather was too "bad" to fly, I would drive my car up. I could then enjoy fishing, hunting and swimming in the summer, ice skating, and downhill skiing at Sheltered Valley Ski Resort in the winter. I would also do snow-shoeing and cross country skiing.

Figure 41: Al at Sheltered Valley Ski Resort in Three Lakes.

I was quite athletic back then. But I have to say, that my first love was and is flying.

Figure 39: A PA-12 airplane which I flew up to Three Lakes, Wisconsin

They closed old Brown Deer Airport to use it for a housing development, so I started flying out of Capitol Drive Airport. I was flying up to Three Lakes to our cabin on Lone Stone Lake every weekend. I decided I needed a float plane which would make it easier for me to get closer to our cabin. So I bought a four-place Aeronca Sedan aircraft and then purchased some floats from a man in Rhode Island and installed them onto the airplane.

Figure 40: An Aeronca Sedan on floats.

At that time a company called Edo Floats, was the largest provider of floats for airplanes, I ordered a booklet from them called "Flying Floats". I read this over and over until I actually had it memorized. I realized I would have to fly the airplane off of a grass airstrip at Capitol Drive Airport. So I then had to build a trailer to put the float plane on to move it. My theory was, that if I could use a car to pull the trailer with the Aeronca Sedan Airplane on it, and get up to sixty miles per hour by the end of the runway, I would have enough flying speed to get the airplane airborne. Which is what happened.

I then flew it to Pewaukee Lake and started practicing flying floats. I followed everything that was described in the Edo Floats booklet. After I had about ten hours of practice flying floats, I contacted the FAA for a flight test so I could get a Commercial Float Plane rating, and if I do say so myself, I passed with "flying colors".

I then flew my float plane to the Three Lakes Airport, which had a large lake on both sides of it (Moccasin and Big Stone). I landed on Big Stone Lake, parked the plane and tied it up on the beach, on the north edge of the airport. I then got someone to drive me back down to Milwaukee where I could then fly my other plane, a Piper PA-12 back to the Three Lakes Airport and land on the airport. Then I got back into my float plane and flew over to our cabin on Lone Stone Lake. This arrangement made it very easy for me to fly my float plane any time I wished.

After a few years, I and my brother Carl purchased some property on Moccasin Lake in Three Lakes, as it was connected to the airport. That fall I stayed in Three Lakes and started building. It took me two years to build a two- bedroom house and a small housekeeping resort during the winter months. In the summer I started giving twenty minute rides in my seaplane, and that was the start of, Hartwig Flying Service and Resort.

After I got out of the National Guards in 1956, during that summer, my brother Carl took up scuba diving, and he had run out of air for his scuba tank. We were west of Rhinelander, Wisconsin and we happened to stop into this little farm to inquire where we could get his tanks filled. A pretty young girl around the age of sixteen came out to the car and talked to us and gave us the information we needed. I have to say that she "peeked" my interest, but I figured she was just too young. After we drove away that day, I found myself thinking of her now and then but could not think of a real good reason to go back and see her.

Oh well, I had a business to run and flying to do, girls could wait.

Hartwigs Build Marina, Flying Busines at Three Lakes After South Am. Stint

A News paper article about Al and his brother, Carl when they started Hartwig Flying Service.

Notice: the sign saying, Hartwig Aero Marine on top of the building roof, this was Carl's part of the business.

The Hartwig brothers, Carl and Al, have been flying since 1948 and have flown all over the world. Since 1951 they have flown commercially out of Milwaukee and for a couple of years flew supplies into diamond mines in South America.

Following their stay in South America the two brothers moved to Three Lakes where they decided to build their flying business. They came to Three Lakes in 1958 and flew charters and guided rides in the area when they fir arrived here.

Flying in South America is quite different from the type of flying done in this area, commented Carl. Often flying in bad weather and over heavy jungle terrain, most of which was unchartered, the brothers flew supplies into the diamond mines in the brush country of South America. The landing fields were unlike those in the states, level and straight. Many of the landing strips layed out for the diamond mines were tilted on the side of a mountain and were dangerous to land on.

During the time they were flying into the mines Castro was becoming very active and they had a chance to fly both for Castro and the free Cubans but decided not to fly for either side and left the country to move to northern Wisconsin.

Carl noted that they could have made as much as $500 for one bombing run flying for the Cubans but they felt it was safer not to get involved in that type of operation.

When they moved to this area they built a home on Moccasin lake next to the Three Lakes airport which allowed them to be close to their business. Prior to moving to Three Lakes they had spent many summers in the lakes region during their off time and before they went to South America.

Since coming to the area and opening their flying service they have greatly expanded their operations to take in all kinds of flying. Two years ago the Hartwig

Aero Marine on Big Stone lake was opened. Carl noted that up to the time of opening the marine service they worked strictly on the flying business. Now the two are separate businesses with Carl in charge of the marina and Al managing the flying service. Within a short time the marina greatly expanded and now offers rentals of boats, motors, water skis, Honda motor bikes and cars. In the winter Carl is kept busy selling and taking care of snowmobiles, which has become a big business in the Headwaters area within the last few years.

During the winter Al is kept busy making chartered flights around the state and taking people hunting and skiing all over the midwest and Canada. Al noted that this winter he will be busy instructing his flying students but will be available for charter jobs. He also makes three to four trips each spring and fall up to Canada for hunting and fishing jobs. He is also the only pilot in northern Wisconsin with a Canadian airtaxi license.

Al is also the only instructor in the northern half of the state that is qualified in the single, multi-engine, seaplane, either and ground school instructions. Carl noted that there are many qualified flying instructors in the area but none of them can teach all the things for which Al has a license.

Hartwig Flying Service has a complete aviation shop for repair of planes. He noted that they possibly have the busiest seaplane shop in the state. The Flying Service also has a number of planes that are always ready for use on chartered flights or for instructions.

The two brothers were born and raised in Cedarburg, Wisconsin and after high school went to Brown Deer airport in 1948 to take flying instructions. After the two received their licenses they went into flying commercially from Milwaukee.

Chapter Eight

Flying High and Busy

During this time, I also flew the editor of the Rhinelander newspaper, who was a steady customer. I would fly him to "flash news points" in northern Wisconsin and northern Michigan.

On one of these trips, when the editor was going to interview a bank official in northern Michigan; who had been robbed a few hours before. The bank official was able to give the news paper editor the color, and the type of get-away vehicle that was used, as well as the license plate number.

After interviewing the bank official, he got back into the airplane and told me to fly as low as I could, while he tried to spot the vehicle which happened to be a white pick-up truck. Well, we "spotted" several white pick-up trucks (but none were the one we were looking for), but we kept looking and in fact we spent several hours doing so.

Finally, I had to tell him that I was getting "low" on fuel and we would have to turn back so I could gas up again. The editor turned and asked me, "can't you just land and gas up at a service station"? I thought about it for a moment, after all I didn't want to lose the extra charter hours I would lose by going back to Three Lakes to gas up, so I looked for a service station which was near the highway where I could taxi up to and re-fuel.

I "spotted" one, landed gassed-up and took off again to keep looking for the truck (which we never did find) but I got an extra three hour charter for doing this. I took out my payment in advertising for my flying business.

As I said, I flew many different reporters and journalists even in the winter months. Iron Mountain, Michigan was always good for a trip in the winter. In those days all the ski-jumpers who were trying out for the

Olympics, would go there to practice and have ski-jumping competitions; and there was always a sports writer/reporter who would want to interview them. The reporters would have me fly them there rather than taking a lot of time driving.

I have to say, it was quite something to see a guy on skis "jump" almost as high as I was flying, as well as getting to see some great ski jumping, also my customers were able to get some pretty good pictures of the "jumping". After the reporter had finished interviewing the ski-jumpers and had taken some pictures, I would fly him back to the Three Lakes Airport where he would again get his car and head back home.

While I was giving seaplanes rides for a living, I would always be on the lookout for lakes that did not have any cabins or cottages on them. If I saw one, I would make a mental note of the lake and then when I had time, I would fly back to the lake, land, get out, stand on the floats and make a few casts. If I caught a fish or at least got a few "bites", I would then bring back a canoe on my floats and pull the canoe up on the shore. I could then bring fishermen early in the morning to have a day's fishing on that lake and I would pick them up that evening.

Well one of these times when I was flying around northern Wisconsin, up near the Michigan border during my "off" season, I spotted a couple of "good looking" likely lakes. I landed and made a few casts and got some real good Bass fishing action! I figured that this would be a "good spot" to bring some of my fishing customers. All of a sudden, I saw a boat heading towards me with some "tough" looking guys in it. They pulled up alongside of my plane and told me that I would have to leave immediately, as this was all "private property", so I left, but thought that it just might be that particular lake.

About a week later, while up in that same area, I spotted another lake near the Wisconsin border, I landed my seaplane and tried another few casts. Again, a boat load of guys came over to my plane and told me to leave, as this was private property. Again I left thinking this was very strange, as all "bodies" of water were supposed to be available to everyone.

In the fall of that year, during one of my charters flying a newspaper journalist around, and flying back from Upper Michigan, as I neared the Wisconsin border, I mentioned to him that all of the lakes below us were private and that no one was allowed on them. He replied, "That it was impossible, for a person to be "kicked-off" any open body of water and he wanted me to show him."

So I saw a lake, landed the seaplane, and a boat came running over to the plane, this time it was three different very tough looking men carrying shot guns. They spoke very abusively, and told us to leave or they would "ram" my floats and sink the plane. The reporter with me, tried to "talk" to them, but they said that this was the third time I had landed on one of these private lakes and this would be the last time it would happen. So we "took off". The Journalist said, "He couldn't believe that something like this could happen in the U.S."

I figured that was the end of it, I had other concerns such as making a living flying! The following spring, the journalist whom I had flown the previous fall, called me for another charter to the Upper Peninsula of Michigan. As we were flying, he asked if I had heard the news. I asked him what news? He told me that he had written a local article about the experience he'd had had landing on that lake with me and being "chased off". He said that the article had gone international and that the U.S. Congress was going to put a "stop" to it, and there would no longer be any "private lakes", now everyone would be able to use any lake in the U.S.

After that, I flew many fishermen into these lakes. I would drop them off for a day's Bass fishing and would go back and pick them up in the evening (which was a twenty minute flight from Three Lakes). On some lakes, I would have boats located for use, and on others I would just use inflated rubber rafts which would take a little time to inflate but worked quite well.

Here is a little history about the property these lakes were on, that I had the experience with.

Back then, it was known as the Sylvania Properties and was used as an exclusive resort for a small number of affluent personages. It was also rumored that it was owned by Fisher Body and General Motors; it was even said that President Eisenhower and foreign dignitaries were invited to stay there.

But I am getting a little ahead of my story; Sylvania Wilderness as it is now known is located a few miles west of Watersmeet, Michigan and is entirely located within the bounds of the Ottawa National Forest, and is currently being managed as a wilderness area as part of the National Wilderness Preservation System by the U.S. Forest Service.

Not much is known about the area prior to the late 1800's other than that the area was used by different clans of Ojibwa Natives, because of the scattered artifacts which were found there. Anyway, in 1895 a lumberman from Wisconsin by the name of A. D. Johnston purchased around eighty acres of land on the end of Clark Lake, which he intended to log all of the large pine trees that were there.

Well, after seeing the land he was so taken by the rugged beauty of it that he changed his mind and decided to preserve it instead. He brought some of his friends up there to see it and many of them were so impressed that they also decided to purchase lands adjacent to his.

They built cabins and lodges on the larger lakes and offered fishing, hunting and hiking as the main things to do. They called it the "Sylvania Club" and used it as a private exclusive resort where they could entertain wealthy influential guests.

Ownership changed hands many times over the years, but was finally purchased by the United States Forest Service in 1967, and they promptly removed all buildings and began to manage it as a special recreation area, and was finally designated as a federal wilderness when the Michigan Wilderness Act was passed by Congress and signed into law by President

Ronald Reagan.

Figure 42: Map of the Apostle Islands in Lake Superior, where I flew tourists up to their summer homes located there.

Figure 43: My Aeronca Sedan on floats that I used to fly tourists to the Apostle Islands.

Chapter Nine

Hartwig Flying Service & Resort

In the summer, I would also fly charters to the Apostle Islands in Lake Superior with my seaplane. Some of these charters were for business, but most of them were with families and couples who were vacationing up there at one of the tourist cottages or in one of the hotels.

There were also many times when I would fly the husband/father back and forth so he could be there on weekends with his family. He would fly to Three Lakes with his airplane on Friday, and would charter me to fly him up there in my seaplane. Then I would return and pick him up on Sunday and bring him back to Three Lakes and his aircraft which he would then fly home to Chicago or Milwaukee.

I had such a good reputation as a safe pilot that this gave me the opportunity of flying several governors of the State of Wisconsin, even though they had their own private airplanes. When they would fly into a community that did not have an airport, they would charter me to fly them in my seaplane.

I was always looking for ways to make a living in aviation; one of the ways was to fly sky-divers. In the fall while the weather was still nice and I didn't have a student, I would fly the "jumpers" and their equipment and they would sky-dive over the Three Lakes Airport.

I always thought I would like to try sky-diving once, but I figured it would be just my luck to break a leg or something else and then I would be laid up and not able to fly or make a living so I never tried it.

Another thing that I did, was airplane maintenance in the winter months. This would consist of doing complete major overhauls and repairs, I would rebuild airplane engines, and airframes, I also completely rebuilt airplane floats; and repaired airplane fuel cells (rubber gas tanks), as well as recovering fabric-covered aircraft. The customers I had came from as far away as Chicago and Milwaukee and all "points" in between.

During this time, I would put my Cub on skis and used during the winter when I couldn't fly a seaplane. I could land my Cub anywhere there was snow, fields, frozen lakes etc., it was a nice little plane to "play" in. (In fact, I have to tell you that after I met Del, who became my future wife, I actually courted her in it.)

Figure 44: The Cub which I would put on skis and fly during the winter months for fun. I also used this plane to court my future wife, Del.

This was also a good airplane when teaching a student to fly. A "Cub", has only two seats, one in front of the other in the back and you use a "stick" and your rudders instead of a "steering type" wheel as in my other airplanes.

Around the middle of the 1950's, my mother and brother moved up to Three Lakes to join me; as by that time I had the two-bedroom house built and ready to live in. During the summer months, we would move into a small cabin down by the lake across from my seaplane base and rent out the two-bedroom house and two twin-duplexes I had built; these three buildings made-up my small housekeeping resort.

Around 1957/58, I realized that we would need a permanent facility for the business as we were getting a lot of customers around this time. I thought about it for a while, and after talking it over with my brother Carl, I decided that we would have a marina, because of all of the boats in the area, and a hangar for my seaplane as well.

I drew up floor plans to build a seaplane hangar with an attached marina and living quarters above. The facility would have places my seaplane customers to sit while they waited and also washrooms; and because of all the boating activity in the area, Carl would be able to sell fishing boats, motors, gas, marine supplies, fishing rods, live baits, fishing lures etc., that would be needed.

I knew this was going to be a challenge, so again I found someone who could give me some information on how to get "footings" for the seaplane hangar down under the water into the sand and make it solid enough to withstand the ice-break-up in the spring.

A famous baseball player from the 1940's retired to the Three Lakes area and had a lumber yard called "Cy Williams Lumber", so I went over and talked to him about this problem, he explained how to do it and we started building in the fall of 1959.

I built some "forms" which were two feet wide by ten feet deep, I then used a "jet pump" to blow the sand away under the water so that I could "sink" the forms four feet deep in the sand. Then I used the "pump" to blow all the sand out of the forms to clear them, so that the "chute" from the cement truck could pour cement into the forms. The cement filled the forms from the bottom to the top, and by doing this, the water was "pushed out" on top until the forms were filled with cement, making this a very solid structure that would with stand the ice breaking-up in the spring.

This was built on the south shore of Big Stone Lake and Highway 32, which was about sixty feet in front of our building and directly across the road from the Three Lakes Airport.

In 1960, I and my brother Carl were still building the marina and seaplane hangar to use during the summer months. It was during this summer that I met the girl who became my wife and was very surprised to find that she was the same pretty young girl who had given us the information on where to get air for my brother's scuba tanks. She was working at the Northernaire Hotel & Resort as a waitress, which was about one half mile from my seaplane base where I was giving rides.

One day that fall while I was outside working on the seaplane hangar, I was actually hack-sawing a reed bar, (which are reinforcing metal rods that are required to be put in concrete footings), well anyway, I guess, I wasn't paying attention to what I was doing, but rather watching Del and I almost sawed my thumb off because of it.

She insisted on taking me to the hospital, but I told her to drive me up to my house instead, so I could bandage my thumb. Yeah, I know, I should have gone to a hospital to have it "looked" at, but I didn't want to waste the time to drive the twenty miles it would take to get there, so we just took care of it at home. I guess, this did work out all right though, as she then had a chance to meet my mother.

Well we were married in the spring of 1961, and after a short three-day honeymoon, she agreed to become my business partner, after all she could type!

Figure 45 & 46: A picture of Del, she became my life partner .

She started right in helping in our business, writing letters to guests, making resort reservations, taking deposits, cleaning cabins, fueling airplanes that landed at the Three Lakes Airport and "selling rides" for me. Sometimes, she went with me, when I went to resorts to pick up passengers. After all, I had the most important job, flying the seaplane!!

We stayed that first summer, upstairs over the marina and seaplane hanger, in a room with bare studs and flooring (we moved out of the two-bedroom house, so we could rent it out in the summer), we slept in a single bed for several months, and took our baths at night in the lake.

Del got pregnant with our first child that summer, and to say that she was sick, would be putting it mildly, actually she was sick both day and night. After one of her doctor's appointments, the doctor told us that there was a new drug that many women were taking and having good success with in stopping "morning sickness". Del wanted to take it, but I said, "No, absolutely not"! I have to say, that this was our first real argument.

I can't really tell you why I felt so strongly about her not taking the drug, but I felt that if she took it, something bad would happen. Anyway, Del finally agreed and we were very glad that I had won the argument; the drug that she had been offered was, Thalidomide, and parents were finding that their children were born badly deformed. Some without arms and only "stumps" of fingers sticking out of their shoulders, or legs without feet only toes.

I have always felt that the less "medicine/drugs" you take, especially if you can actually use an alternative method or get by without it, that it is better for you. I wouldn't even take and aspirin until just the last few years.

That fall, after we had moved back to our home, I and Carl were working on the building down by the lake; when this incident happened. I have to say it was a little "unsettling". Now I have been around animals and a hunter all of my life, but I have never seen anything like this.

I and Carl were working outside, when Carl shouted for me to turn around. I did and saw this raccoon heading towards me. Its fur was very matted and it was "foaming" at the mouth, it looked sick. We tried to "scare" it off, but it just kept coming at us and growling. Finally I ran back into the building and grabbed a gun and shot it. I then called the DNR and told them what had happened.

They told me not to touch it in anyway because it was probably "rabid". This was a little disconcerting, as where we lived, there were woods all around and many raccoons, squirrels and foxes, all of which can get rabies. I never saw any other cases, but heard that it was very prevalent that year.

Okay back to business, during the day I gave twenty minute seaplane rides and taught students to fly an airplane in the evenings. While giving seaplane rides at Three Lakes, I would be able to make three "rides" an hour with from three to five adults per each ride. In an average summer seaplane ride season, I would "log" a minimum of five to six hundred hours on just one seaplane that I used for giving rides in fact, I even "ate" my lunch while flying passengers.

For the charters, I used a Cessna 206 on floats, a Piper 250 Comanche aircraft on wheels and a 260 Navion aircraft on wheels.

At one time I had: a Piper Tripacer, a Piper Cub, two Aeronca Sedan seaplanes, a Cessna 206 seaplane, a Piper 250 Comanche, a Piper Colt, and a 260 Navion. I also rented a Cessna 185 seaplane and had a Cessna twin engine "Bamboo Bomber" for rebuilding.

That fall, we got a distributorship to sell Piper Aircraft and so I purchased a Piper Colt, which we flew to Palm Beach Florida to attend a Piper Aircraft Convention. They said that we flew the farthest in the smallest aircraft with the biggest amount of luggage (I think Del packed everything we owned)! Later we sold the Colt. While at the convention, I had the opportunity to meet Mr. Piper himself, who founded and owned the Piper Aircraft Company (he was in his nineties at the time).

We met a couple who owned a flying business during the convention. The lady was a flight instructor. They were very good friends of the owners of Rahr Malting Company and were staying at their friends house.

She took a real liking to Del, and they invited us to come over and visit with them at the house they were using, knowing that Del was pregnant and they were going to be leaving soon, they made arrangements for us to stay in the house after they left.

We couldn't get over the place. It was "huge", and even had "gold" bathroom fixtures on the sink, in the large Jacuzzi bathtub and shower. The place also had a king sized round bed (there were no king size beds at that time), and the best thing of all, it was located only five blocks from President Kennedy's vacation place down there.

Wow, talk about "living high on the hog"!!

Figure 48: An aerial view of the Three Lakes Airport, the marina I built on the lake. The hangar and airport office I built on the airport and on the right you can see our home and resort (in the trees) and to the right of the trees, in the clearing, are the two pre-fab houses I built and sold.

Chapter Ten

More Adventures

The fall that "Butch" was just learning to walk, I heard that Milwaukee was selling houses that had to be removed or destroyed, so that a new super highway could be put through the city. I heard that some of them were "pre-fab" houses, (a "pre-fab" type house is one that is already made; you just have to "put" it together rather than building it from "scratch").

Figure 47: Thanksgiving dinner in our "new" pre-fab house in 1964. At the table is Del on the left, Karla our daughter (1 yr. old), "Butch" (2 ½ yrs old) and my mother on the right.

Del, I and Butch drove down to Milwaukee so that I could try and purchase a couple if these houses at a property auction. The pre-fab houses were the only ones that were being sold, as they could be disassembled, removed and reassembled on another property. I figured I could "rebuild" them back in Three Lakes.

Well I bought three of them no problem, the only "catch" to it was, I had to take them down myself which really was no "big deal". I would go everyday and work at disassembling them. While I was working on the last house, I started to feel real "light-headed" and weak, in fact while carrying a large section of the house, I fell to my knees. I was not sure what was wrong but, I figured that I had better get home soon. I loaded the last of it and took it to be stored at my brother, Max's place.

Bass Fishing From the Sky

By TOM GUYANT, of The Journal Staff

THREE LAKES, Wis. — Beneath the plane, the pines and tamaracks pointed skyward like a million church spires. This greenery was dotted with lakes and the lakes were specked with islands. On the hazy horizon, a long, narrow lake cut a canyon in the trees. Al Hartwig aimed the seaplane at this strip of blue.

We were heading into Michigan's Upper Peninsula. Hartwig had a notion that bass would bite in one of the little wilderness lakes just north of the state line.

Hartwig is a transplanted Milwaukeean who likes to fish and who likes to fly. Combining the two, he has discovered small patches of water accessible only by air and scarcely large enough to drop down and take off with a pontoon equipped plane.

The Man Does Bragging

The day before, Hartwig had put his plane down on the lake where Bill Hoeft and I were fishing. Hoeft, the man who wakes farmers each morning on WTMJ, hadn't caught a fish. Hartwig thought he could cure this.

"You won't believe it, but I know a lake where we get bass on every other cast," Hartwig had said.

Such bragging cannot go unchecked. Next day shortly after dawn, Hartwig set his plane down on the Eagle chain where we were staying. Rods were stashed in the baggage compartment and we transferred bass lures from big tackle boxes to pocket size containers. I stuck a bottle of pork frogs in one pocket.

It was a 20 minute flight to the lake, one of hundreds of unnamed puddles just north of Land O' Lakes, just over the line into Michigan's timbered wilderness.

Hartwig made a pass over the lake. We were just above the treetops, and in the shallows of the lake were hundreds of bass nests, sandy circles along the weedy shore.

The plane splashed down. Hartwig gunned the motor and moved the craft toward a rocky shore. It was hot, but the blast from the propeller shot cool air into our faces when Hartwig opened the doors and we scrambled out onto the pontoons and cast.

Water Is Glass Clear

Fallen trees thrust out into the shallows. The water was clear and we could see the lures 50 feet away, see the bass as they came out from beneath the logs.

We stood on the pontoons to fish. Hartwig kept the plane in position with a little paddle.

"I'm going to get a collapsible canoe and haul it along," Hartwig said. "Last year we used rubber rafts, but they're hard to inflate and hard to fish from. I've got boats stationed on some of the lakes."

It took a few minutes to find the right lure. I stuck a pork chunk on a weedless spoon and caught three bass on three casts. Hoeft trimmed up his lure in a similar way and the action was unbelievable. Sometimes, five or six bass would chase a lure.

So clear was the water that we could set the hook by sight, not feel. But the fish soon spooked. Then Hartwig would gun the motor and move us to another bay.

On each move, we grabbed a wing strut, rode the pontoons and motor trolled. Two big bass were caught that way. Motor trolling is legal in Michigan.

25 Bass in Hour

Most of the bass were in the one and two pound class, but Hoeft hooked a five pounder and, on the last cast before we left, I caught one about the same size that came up out of nowhere and bit the spoon right next to the plane. All told, we caught and released some 25 bass in an hour.

There were more lakes to look at, so we buckled our seat belts. Hartwig gunned the motor, taxied down the lake. Spray flew. The shore line spun past, disappeared as the plane climbed.

Below us were the trees and lakes, marshes and bogs and curling little rivers. And behind us was the little lake with the big supply of bass.

Figure 50: A newspaper article that was written by Tom Guyant of the Milwaukee Journal.

Chapter Eleven

New Challenges

I re-built two of the "pre-fab" houses on the new property I had purchased on Moccasin Lake. One I got ready immediately so that my growing family could live there; as I told you before, we moved out every summer and rented our house and twin duplexes for a housekeeping resort every summer; so I needed a place for my family

The winter of 1964, I got a job flying guests for the Stevens Point Asphalt Products Company. They hired me to fly their guests, one month in the spring, one month in the fall to their lodge on Big Stone Lake (there was no road into it). I flew out of Red Lake, Ontario (which was a small town at the end of Highway 105). It was also agreed, that when the camp was not being used for their guests, I could use the camp for any customers I had, for some good Canadian fishing and hunting; this also added to my flying business.

Near the end of that October, I flew a couple of guys up to an outpost north of Red Lake. Bill Froelich, from Sayner, Wisconsin who wanted to shoot a "trophy" moose for his lodge in Sayner; and Robert Hermann, the son of the president of Georgia Marietta Corporation from Fort Lauderdale, Florida who was more interested in getting a "good camera hunt".

They would have me "aerial spot" trophy moose by plane, (it was completely legal back then to aerial "spot" game), anyway, when we spotted a large moose, I would land the seaplane "down-wind" and using the "stalking" technique that Fred "Papa" Bear had shown me, I would have the hunters follow until we were within shooting range; then I would sit down and let the hunters continue on using the technique I had shown them, until they got their "camera shot" or kill.

Figure 51: Bill Froelich, I and another man with Bill's trophy moose.

Figures 52: Al loading the trophy moose head on the airplane float.

Figure 52: Al with his float plane.

I am happy to say, that the moose Froelich shot was a beauty and it "tipped" the scale at a nice two thousand pounds with and antler spread of fifty-four inches. In fact it was so large, that it took me two trips to bring the carcass and "rack" back to the outpost camp.

We saw so many animals, that Hermann was able to get many very good pictures. I can say for sure, that both men were very pleased with their trip.

My hunters always got what they were looking for, and I ended up getting such a good reputation for doing this, that I had hunters come even from the Boone & Crockett Club (this is an organization that records the largest game obtained by hunters) to book moose hunting charters with me to get a trophy moose.

I would show my hunting clients the "stalking" tricks that I had learned from Fred Bear the famous bow hunting authority.

Deer Lake was the area I liked for taking my hunting customers, it is north of Red Lake, Ontario. I would fly all day about fifty air miles further north of Deer Lake, and then I would return my hunters to Red Lake for "nicer sleeping" accommodations. To do this, I had to have aviation fuel stored at Deer Lake.

I would fill the "step" compartments of the aircraft floats with aviation fuel,(because the fuel in the floats is below the aircraft), I would haul close to two hundred gallons at a time up to Deer Lake where I would store the fuel in fifty gallon drums.

Now every float plane pilot has a "float pump", this is a hand operated pump like an old air tire pump; you simply remove the cover from the circular hole on top of the float and insert the pump into the hole which has a tube running to the bottom of the floats, (the pump is usually used to pump any water out of the floats), I also used it to pump the fuel that I was carrying as well.

Again, I used my "trick" of the "felt hat filter" in the funnel when I

Figure 54: Me with my seaplane

Figure 55: Another article about fishing for bass.

Canada isn't the only place where a man can fly in to fish. Wilderness lakes of northern Wisconsin and upper Michigan provide fishing sites for a handful of bush pilots. Some of the lakes have no roads for access; some are ringed by private property. Airplanes equipped with pontoons can land on them. Al Hartwig of Three Lakes, a seaplane pilot, loads his plane in preparation for such a flight, then, standing on the plane, holds up a bass caught from a small, secluded lake just north of Land o' Lakes.

Figure 56: Removing the floats from my Aeronca Sedan.

gassed the airplane.

The "felt hat filter" blocked any debris or water that went into the tanks. On one of my "fuel" hauls to Deer Lake, I had "glass like" water surface, no wind at all. The temperature also was quite warm which made it very hard to gain flying speed. I made several attempts to get the floats "up on the step" (this is like getting a speed boat up on top of the water so that it can "plane" on the surface). Finally I was able to get the seaplane floats to "plane" on the lake's surface, but I still could not gain enough flying speed.

I slowly "raised" one float out of the water and was only "riding" on one float, but I still could not get that little bit more speed needed to become airborne. I slowly made a large circle -turn on the lake until I could "hit" one of the waves that I had made with the one float I still had in the water, and "Bang" I was airborne!

When I returned to Red Lake that evening Del, told me that the entire Howey Bay seaplane fraternity had been watching me, as they all thought that I was going to "flip" the seaplane over. No one had ever seen anyone do that with a seaplane.

That is when I realized that not one of the forty or fifty seaplane pilots at Red Lake had a "clue" of the different ways to fly floats.

When I originally got my seaplane rating and started flying seaplanes, an "old timer" showed me how to do "figure eights" on a lake as well as many other "tricks". By learning to fly on either float, a pilot can land or take off on a river that has many turns and bends in it.

You simply get "on the step" and if the river turns left, you "roll" the aircraft up on the left float. If the river then turns right, you "roll" the aircraft up onto the right float, you keep doing this until you have enough flying speed and then Away You Go!!

If a lake is large enough to land on by using the above technique, you can

Figure 57 & 58: some advertising for
Hartwig Air Service.

safely take off as well. For example: the aircraft is taxied to the downwind shore line, then you head the aircraft into the wind to get the floats to "plane" (get up on the step), you are now almost on the opposite shore line, so you "roll "the floats onto the left float, circle the lake from where you started and then just as you head back into the wind, add full power and you will become airborne. You climb into the wind and start a climbing left turn; all of the time staying over the lake, (you can make another round if necessary). If you are above the trees by a good margin you just keep going up over the trees.

I have found that most flying accidents with a seaplane are when climbing out of a lake too close to the trees, because there is always a "down draft" over these trees going into the lake which a "low flying" seaplane cannot out climb of.

Okay, a little on the lighter side. While we were living in Red Lake we were renting a mobile home on Howey Bay Road and became very good friends with an airplane mechanic named Vic Sarapu and his wife Julie. They had a couple of little girls and our children used to play with them; also Del and Julie spent a lot of time together. One day, the weather was bad, (the clouds were too low and it looked like it might rain).

All of the seaplanes were just sitting there, no one was flying. I thought I might as well head home and have lunch with my family. When I got home, I noticed that there were a lot of cars next door and Del and the kids were gone. So I headed over to Vic and Julie's place and found a houseful of pilots having a "party". They asked me if I would like a drink? I told them that I better not, in case the weather cleared and I could fly.

They then offered me a "cider" and I figured it was "apple cider", so I said, "Yes." After I had had a couple of glasses of the "cider", I was starting to feel a "little wobbly" and I asked them what kind of apple cider this was. Vic informed me it was "hard cider" not just apple cider juice which I was expecting. Needless to say, I didn't go flying that day after all!!

That fall when I and my family got back to Three Lakes, I started to build a hanger and office with an attached two bedroom apartment, (the office and apartment were actually one of the pre-fab houses I had purchased in Milwaukee), on the Three Lakes Airport and moved my family into the attached apartment.

The back of the hangar, I used to do airplane maintenance during the winter months. The charter airplane was parked in the front section, which had a large over-head door that could be opened to allow an airplane to be brought into the maintenance part.

Our lives were quite busy. I flew for Stevens Point Asphalt Products for two months each year, gave seaplane rides all summer, taught students in the evenings and after dark. I did airplane charters and flew fisherman and hunters up to Red Lake when not flying for Stevens Point Asphalt Products. Del took care of the rest; and in January of 1965 gave birth to our third child, this time another boy that we named Erich.

While I'm thinking about it, I have to tell you a "little" story concerning Del before I continue on. You see, it was in the late fall of the year and Del needed a doctor's check-up. She was very busy with the then three children and the business. She asked me to make the appointment for her. I agreed, and the following week Del, I and our three young children drove down to Rhinelander.

When Del went in to keep her appointment and gave her name, the nurse began to laugh. Del looked over at me kind of puzzled, I guess I looked a little embarrassed, especially when the nurse said to Del, "Oh, you are the one who is here for a front-end inspection". I have to say, Del was not too happy with the situation or me at that moment.

But in my defense, I couldn't think of the right word to use for her check-up appointment.

Okay, let's go on. We also "acquired" a couple of other "things" as well. One of them was a donkey, yes, I said a donkey. Her name was "Molly". I bought her as an added attraction for the resort, the resort guests would ride her and she was quite gentle but a "real clown". For instance, when she got tired of giving rides, she would walk real close to something and of course the person sitting on her back would lean over a "little" and would then just slide–off her back. She would stop and turn and look down at them as though to ask, "what are you doing down there?"

Another of her "tricks", was when the people from the resort would ask to ride her, she would "act" as though something was wrong. She would drop her head and stumble a little bit. The customers would then go and get Del in the house (office) to inform her that "something was wrong" with the donkey. Del would then have to go out and "see" what the problem was. It usually took only for Del to speak to "Molly" and say, "that's enough, behave yourself", and she would all of a sudden "perk" up and start to trot around with the customers. But the guests really enjoyed riding that donkey.

Figure 59: This is a picture of "Molly", a donkey which we got for our resort guests to ride.

There was also an otter that we made a "pet" of. He had been injured by a boat propeller and ended up lying on the dock of the seaplane hangar. We would feed him dead minnows each day, (Carl sold minnows at the marina which was attached to my seaplane hangar). The otter got better and decided he "liked being taken care of" and became tame enough that you could even handle him.

He also was very curious. One day he went upstairs to the apartment, where my brother Carl and his wife were living, to have a look around. Carl and Nancy had just had a baby who was sleeping in a bassinette in the nursery. The baby made a small sound, so the otter just had to go and "check" it out. He actually stood up on his hind-legs to "peek" into the bassinette where the baby was sleeping.

Figure 60: A picture of the otter which had been injured by a boat prop, we fed and made a pet of.

It quickly became a normal thing for the otter to go up stairs every day, and Carl and Nancy would leave pieces of hamburger for him in a small dish in the refrigerator. The otter could even open the refrigerator with his paw and get his dish of hamburger. We enjoyed having him around for several years.

The DNR tried several times to remove him (they said we couldn't have a "wild" animal as a pet) to other lakes and rivers, but he always came back by us. Finally the DNR took him so very far away that he could not find his way back and we never saw him again.

In 1966, I had the new accommodations ready and Del, and our now three children moved into our new home, so I sold the two other pre-fab houses I had built on Moccasin Lake.

Del now had an actual office to work from. Along with the three small children, she took care of the resort, did resort bookings, answered the telephones and airport Unicom radio, drove the gas truck to gas the airplanes, book charters and student times for me, and generally operated the airport while I was flying or gone on charters.

She took the children along with her when she brought my lunch to the plane, while I was giving seaplane rides. She also would take my mother grocery shopping or to church whenever asked.

I had gotten my Pilot Instructor's license in the 1950's and had been teaching pilots to fly for around ten or so years. Now one thing that all Pilot Instructors have to do to keep their instructor's rating, is to attend a FAA Seminar. In October of 1966 while attending one of these seminars, the FAA wanted the pilots to do a test flight (you see, the idea for this was so that all flight instructors were teaching flying maneuvers the same way), on this day the weather was very "nasty" with the winds gusting very hard and we had to take off flying into a "cross-wind." No one wanted to fly that day, but I volunteered to take the flight test. So with a FAA Examiner beside me and four flight instructors behind me in the airplane we took-off. I did all of the maneuvers they asked me to perform, finally the FAA Examiner asked if I wanted to "cut" the flight test short because of the extreme weather conditions. I told them not necessarily, as I did not have any problem flying in cross-wind conditions.

Later that evening, several men and I were discussing flying and the different maneuvers which the FAA wanted us to perform and teach, many of these were actually wrong as I had proven while flying myself. One of the men standing near us turned and asked me what I thought of the FAA. Fortunately or unfortunately, I told him! The next thing I knew he said, "congratulations, you are now a FAA Examiner." Boy, that was sure a surprise to me, and that is how I became one of the youngest Flight Examiners the state of Wisconsin ever had. I was thirty-six years old.

Figure 61: The "flyer" advertising we handed out to prospective clients.

Chapter Twelve

Some Memorable Flying Experiences

They say if a person lives long enough, that they will have experienced many different things and situations. Well I guess that is true, so I'm going to take a few moments to recount some of mine. Some have been a little bit of a "nail biter" type and some just plain silly. Oh well anyway, here goes.

I have to tell you about one of my first "scary" experiences. I was in my early twenties and had just rebuilt a Stinson Station Wagon airplane at the old Brown Deer Airport under the supervision of Bob Huggins. I decided to take the plane on a "good long" test flight. Since it was winter in Milwaukee, I figured that the best place to head for, was the warmth of Florida.

So I packed a gym bag the size of a "carry-on" and got into the airplane and left around nine o'clock am in the morning. By about eleven o'clock pm that night, I was flying over the northern part of Florida. When I heard a loud "bang" and started to see a red glow coming from the left side of the cowling. I pulled the "lean out" and shut off the engine, I was flying at about ninety-five hundred feet high. Luckily there was a full moon shining that night, so I "glided" towards what I hoped was an open field where I could make a "safe landing".

When I got over the tops of the trees, I turned on my aircraft landing lights and "side slipped" it into a small field and "stomped" on my brakes. I stopped twenty feet short of a fence! I didn't know exactly where I was, and since it was quite late by now, I simply slept in my airplane that night. The next morning, I took a look at my plane to try and figured out what the problem was. I discovered a burnt valve that had separated and had "blown" the top of a cylinder off.

A little later I saw a farmer coming towards me and asked him for a ride to the nearest airport, which happened to be located on a remote grass airstrip. The man who ran the airstrip said he had a cylinder which he could take off a "scrapped" engine. He told me he would sell it to me for fifty dollars, and then he drove me back to my airplane and helped me put the cylinder on as I did not have any tools with me.

I asked the farmer, if I could pay him to take down a part of his fence so I would have room enough to take off. Then I continued on to St. Petersburg which had been my destination. I spent two to three days there before heading back to Milwaukee.

While I was in St. Petersburg, I felt a little "strange" and out of place. It seemed that where ever I looked I saw "old people", but that was probably because everyone was in their fifties and I was in my late teens, early twenties, and to the "young" everyone over thirty is old!

As I mentioned before, I had a J-3 Cub, a "fun" airplane. One of the things I would do to both sharpen my flying skills and have fun, was to roll out about three feet of toilet paper and then drop the roll out of the Cub airplane. When you dropped the roll it would become a long streamer of paper and you would try to "cut" the paper with the plane as many times as you could until you "ran" out of paper. I know, this was silly, but it was also fun and really sharpened your skills flying.

One of the more embarrassing moments in my flying career, was when Del and I with "Butch", when he was a baby and sleeping in the back seat of our Navion aircraft; we were returning from a trip to Chicago and I was at the end of the runway at O'Hare airport. When I lost air pressure in my propeller dome and couldn't engage the "take-off pitch" (which is like putting your car into low gear), and there were FOUR airliners lined up behind me.

Well, there was nothing else for me to do, but get out and manually turn the propeller to a lower pitch, get back into the airplane and continued to take-off and fly home. But to say I felt embarrassed, is saying the least!

91

I have to tell you about one of the students I remember. It was a woman and I don't even remember her name, but I do remember that she wasn't very tall. I guess you could say that she was "short"? Anyway she told me that she was an air force pilot and had been a "test" pilot for them. She also told me that she had flown with one of the acrobatic teams. I am sorry but I do not remember which team it was.

Any way she had come to me to get a seaplane rating. Now the only people I would teach to fly a seaplane, was a pilot with a commercial pilot's rating, because of my knowledge flying seaplanes and the excellent reputation I had for doing so, the FAA sent her to me.

So that she could fly the plane I had to make several adjustments. I added extra cushions to the seat so she could "see" over the dash of the aircraft and some small wooden blocks were fastened onto the rudder pedals, just so she could reach the pedals, but I have to say, that even though she was small, she was sharp! I flew with her for an hour a day for five days and it was no problem at all for her to get her seaplane rating.

Another experience I have to tell you, is when Del was pregnant with our first baby and everything and smell made her feel sick. Well it just so happened, that this one night we had gone to bed and were sleeping, and I got this "strange" feeling that someone was looking at me. I opened my eyes and there was Del, looking down at me with this "odd" look on her face. Finally she said, "do you know, you smell like a stale beer can?"

You see, I had been in the habit of going to the local "watering hole" across the road from the seaplane base for a large schooner of beer when I finished flying for the day. As I would be so very dehydrated from flying all day in the airplane without having anything to drink, that the one large beer seemed to "quench" my thirst. Well, it was the "last" beer I had for the rest of her pregnancy I can tell you.

Then there was the time when we were going to fly down to Milwaukee for a few days. Del had everything packed and the children ready to go as soon as I finished flying for the day. She even had a lunch packed for me to eat while I was flying.

We took off around six o'clock pm and as it got later in our flight, I found that I was having more and more trouble seeing the dials on the flight panel, in fact I was flying on instrument by this time. I said, "what the heck is going on, I can hardly see the instrument dials and I can't see anything at all outside". I asked Del to hand me a flashlight so I could see what was going on. As she turned to hand me the flashlight, she looked at me and asked, "Why are you still wearing your sunglasses"? I had forgotten to take them off after wearing them all day. Boy, talk about feeling "foolish".

Okay, and then there was the time, we were flying back in our Comanche late one night and were preparing to land at the Three Lakes Airport, (which of course was and still is, a grass strip airport). But at that time there were no runway lights and the local deer herd usually enjoyed a late night "snak" on the runway.

As I started to lower the landing gear, all of the lights went out on the dash, I again asked Del to hand me a flashlight, (which was something I usually had with us), and by luck we had one. I turned it on and saw that the master circuit breaker was "tripped". I then proceeded to reset it and was able to get the landing gear down and locked. We made our usual airport handing which was a little "harry" to say the least, because there were no airport lights and deer were always on the runway. I turned the aircraft landing lights on, touched down, "slammed" on the brakes to avoid hitting the deer and Hey, we were home! Just another typical flight!

Then there was one day, when I was flying, and had stopped at a resort on a small lake over in Sugar Camp, Wisconsin. I had a full load of passengers in my seaplane and was taking-off. I had almost "cleared" the tree line when my engine quit, I made a sharp turn as I was still over the lake, and made a perfect landing, but before I came to a stop I felt a "thump" and saw that one of my floats was coming off and the wing tip was almost touching the water. I had hit a "deadhead" (this is a submerged log or stump of a tree). O-kay.

I saw a boat a short distance from me, and called them to come over and help me by putting their boat under my airplane wing. They just sat there looking at me. After calling to them a second time and again they not moving, I started to swear at them. Finally, they seemed to come out of a "shock or trance", (I guess because of seeing the airplane landing like that), but finally they came over and put their boat under the wing tip.

As I started the engine, I noticed that the "knob" for the lean mixture was pulled out, (which is what made the engine quit), I asked the child that was sitting in the front, "if he had touched the knob," he said, "that he had just wanted some cool air". As his father was sitting right beside him, all I could say was, "you Do Not touch things on airplanes without permission"! Anyway, between the men in the boat and my slowly taxing the airplane, we got the seaplane up onto the shore. When I thanked the men who had helped me, I found out they were priests. Talk about making an impression, oh yeah!!

I then found a phone and called Del to get my brother Carl and bring the trailer with the "lift" to help me get the airplane home. She came with the equipment. Between Carl and myself, we removed the wings and floats, put the plane back on wheels, and got the plane up on the trailer with everything. We then drove the ten or twelve miles back to the Three Lakes Airport.

We put the airplane into the hangar where I worked on it all night and had it ready and back in the water the next morning. Later that morning or early afternoon, a TV van, reporters and some radio news announcers arrived and asked us about the airplane accident. We gave them a "wide eyed" look of surprise, and asked them, "what airplane accident"?

After all, this was my lively-hood and with six ads running a day on the radio, news of an airplane accident would have completely "killed" the business for that summer. Like I said before, you do what you have to do.

94

Del and I were listening to TV one evening, when we heard a report that a "bad storm" with very high winds was going to be in the area later that night.

Now I had an agreement with Del, that she would listen for the "sound of bad" weather,(rain on the roof or wind). while we slept. I have to say, Del "came through" again for me. The wind started to blow real hard and she woke me. We got dressed, called my brother and woke him up to help us. Then we drove the big gas truck down to the lake and drove it beneath the wing of the seaplane, where we tied the strut of the wing to the truck. This kept the seaplane from "flipping" over.

When this incident happened, I didn't have a seaplane hangar ready to put the plane into, instead I had to "run" it up onto a ramp down at the lake and park it there for the night.

As I had mentioned before, I only took seaplane students who had their commercial pilot ratings, as it is a challenge just learning to fly an airplane without trying to teach someone to fly a seaplane, which takes a little more experience.

Anyway, this one summer, I had a United Airlines captain with five thousand hours of flying time. If a pilot is "sharp" they can get their seaplane rating in five hours, (this was five days with me, as I could only instruct them when I wasn't doing my own business of flying) well I felt that anyone who had that many hours, (five thousand), should have no problem getting his seaplane rating.

We took off, and I was quite relaxed, I had my seat rolled back and didn't even have my hands near the wheel. I had one arm over the back of the seat, and had "talked" him through what we were going to be doing. We took off, got airborne and "leveled off." I told him to fly over to Columbus Lake as the ceiling (cloud height) was only three to four hundred feet high.

The first thing a student is taught, is when a seaplane stalls (quits flying), that it takes a couple of hundred feet to gain flying speed again. You regain flying speed by lowering the "nose" of the plane, using full power, until you go fast enough that the airplane is again flying.

I told him to "stall" the seaplane to show him, that because of the airfoil-drag of the large floats, you have more altitude loss and need more time to recover. THIS IS A MUST training-exercise for seaplanes, because a land aircraft can make a much quicker recovery.

Anyway, he pulled the nose up but would never completely "stall" the seaplane. On his fourth try at stalling the aircraft, he panicked and "pushed" the control column all the way to the dash board so fast that we became instantly upside down and his hands were "frozen" to the control wheel.

I took my left hand and hit him as hard as I could, so I could regain control of the aircraft. I then did a slow roll to right (the aircraft was now at a very low altitude). As I righted the aircraft, one wing almost touched the lake surface.

What made this extremely "nerve wracking" was that I never had my seat rolled so far back when teaching a student; and this made it extremely difficult to reach the rudder pedals or the control wheel rapidly in case of an emergency.

Now I've given seaplane ratings to astronauts, test pilots, and some very accomplished pilots, but from that day forward, I didn't care what reputation anyone had, I made sure my seat was fully forward and I no longer trusted any novice or professional.

This was the closest I have ever come to being killed in an airplane.

My brother talked me into hiring his wife's brother (his brother-in-law) who was an aircraft mechanic. One of his jobs was to gas the seaplane in between my twenty minute trips. This time after he had gassed the plane, I noticed that there was a "bad" storm coming in, but I knew that I could make one last trip.

So I "hopped" into the seaplane and took off with my passengers. After I was airborne and flying for a "bit", I noticed that my gas gauge seemed to be dropping and when I turned and looked outside towards the back of the plane, I saw the "gas flowing out" the back of the wing and I realized that Stan, had not put the gas cap back on the plane after he had gassed it.

I made a perfect landing on the lake and kept the plane on "the step" (when you do this, the plane acts like a "speed boat") and taxied back towards our dock. I told the passengers we were going to taxi on the water like a boat because the storm was coming in faster than I expected.

The passengers deplaned and thanked me for the "great ride", I told them goodbye; another "problem" successfully taken care of, but I sure was " P O'd" at Carl's brother-in-law.

Usually I did all of my own airplane maintenance, however again, I let Carl talk me into letting his brother-in-law do some work on an airplane for me. I was very reluctant to do this, but Carl assured me that Stan would do a good job as he was a licensed aircraft mechanic.

So I had him do some minor work on the Navion, such as reinstalling the window trim, carpeting, seats and a few control knobs. (I had completely reupholstered the side walls of the plane), so his job was just basically doing "touch up" work.

Of course this was in the fall as that was the only time when it was a little slower and was when I had time to do maintenance and other work on the airplanes. One day we again decided to fly to Milwaukee, Wisconsin. Del packed and got our children and bags ready and over to the airplane.

It was after dark before we could leave, as I had to finish some work on my projects. We took off as usual with no runway lights on the airport and deer feeding on the lush grass. We taxied up and down the runway to "scare them" off and then quickly turned around and took off.

I was airborne for about two minutes and had gained four hundred feet of altitude, when the engine quit "cold". As usual, I started to "swear like a pirate" and quickly turned on the electric fuel boost-pump, this did not help. I then switched to a different gas tank and the engine started to "purr" for all of "Two Minutes" and then again stopped.

By now, I'm really "pissed off" and swearing, I again switched to another gas tank and the engine again ran for about two minutes and then once again quit. I then started looking for a place to land. Thank God, there was a little bit of moon light but the few fields I that could see, were "soaking wet" from a heavy rain we'd had. Because of the muddy condition, I knew we would have to land with the gear up. If the gear was down, we would probably do a lot of damage or even "flip" the aircraft over on to its back, as the nose wheel would sink into the mud.

Anyway, Del is praying and I am swearing and telling Del, "that now that I have my Navion like new, I do not want to go landing in a field". (Of course Del has always said, that it was her prayers that got us safely back on the ground and our destination).

So once again I switched tanks and the engine started to work, I kept switching tanks and headed for Rhinelander, I knew that I couldn't turn around and head back to Three Lakes because there were no runway lights there, and there were also two large lakes on each end of the runway making it a little dangerous to try to return home.

We made it to Rhinelander by switching to each of the four different tanks (I tried them all). I made a smooth landing and spent the night with Del's folks who lived there. The next day, I headed over to the Rhinelander Airport and my beautifully restored Navion and got to work.

Because each of the four gas tanks were only letting two minutes of fuel flow, I figured that the fuel "finger strainers" had to be plugged with some "grit" which I surmised was from a "bad batch" of fuel. (There had been many times I had found this, while doing maintenance on my different customer's aircraft).

So I checked the strainers on all four of the gas tanks, the fuel lines, and the fuel pump and strainer, also the carburetor, but I could not find any problems to cause the "fuel starvation" that I had experienced.

I then started to think of what Stan may have done while working on the interior trim, I checked the "fuel selector" and sure enough, he had put it on wrong! The selector is a knob that turns to the four different positions for each tank and he had placed the "pointer" showing the tank it was to be on, "between" the proper positions so every time I turned the fuel selector knob it "passed" over the proper tank outlet and would stop in between the tanks.

By switching the selector every two minutes, I would get small "bursts" of fuel. I spent TWO days tearing the airplane apart and it was as simple as removing a control knob screw, rotating the knob fifteen degrees and replacing the screw. This small mistake was, and is the REASON, I do not want ANYONE working on my airplane! This kind of mistake could have ended very differently than it did.

I guess I'll now tell you one of the stories of some of my more "dangerous flying experiences", this was while we owned the fishing camp on Gods Lake. Well, unless a pilot is very experienced, qualified and has hundreds of hours in a particular type of aircraft, doing this is truly against ALL flying rules. Because it is seven hundred and thirty air miles round trip from Gods Lake to Winnipeg and return; and there are no aviation fuel stops available anywhere that an airplane on wheels can land and fuel up, you therefore always had to leave with all fuel tanks full.

Now aircraft are tested for the maximum weight they can safely carry, so that they can lose one engine (if it is a multi-engine aircraft) and still be able to continue flying on only one. When I was in Winnipeg getting supplies for the camp, I kept loading my aircraft until I knew that it would just be able to fly. For "example, when using the Twin Beech, I knew that the aircraft would fly if I could raise the tail above the runway to the "level flight" position; and I judged this by, if I could get the tail off the runway in five thousand feet, that the airplane would fly.

Of course, I would only do this if I could take off on runway thirty-one, where the end of it goes over open farm land. With the heavy loads I would carry, runway thirty-one was also the nearest one to where I parked the airplane. I knew that on this runway I only had to taxi several hundred feet to the "take-off" position. So when the tower cleared me for "take-off" and I got the tail in the level flight position (in not more than five thousand feet) I knew that before I reached the end of the runway, I would have "flying speed".

With the heavy loads I carried, I could only "climb" a little over one hundred feet per minute; I also l knew that if I even got a little power loss in either of the engines, I would start to descend. That is why I would not fly over any "built-up" areas.

Now the normal procedure was to raise the gear then immediately raise the flaps, and throttle back when you reached one thousand feet, let the engines "cool" a bit down and then add power to gain a little more altitude. You would do this several times until you had at least thirty-five hundred feet on your altimeter.

Even when reaching Gods Lake and Elk Island, after "burning-off" forty percent of your fuel, you were still so heavy that you had to make a very smooth landing so as not to damage the tail wheel of your aircraft.

The only times I did this, was when I was hauling freight, NEVER when I had passengers,(then I would not go over the legal gross weight for the aircraft).

I remember another memorable trip I made when we had the camp at Elk Island, on one of these trips that I was flying fuel up to Gods Lake. We had purchased a rubber bladder which was four feet by four feet by twelve feet, and when it was empty it could be collapsed and rolled into a small "bundle" that was easy to handle.

When I used it, I would "roll" it out onto the floor of the airplane cabin and have it filled with aviation fuel for the lodge. I think it could hold about five hundred gallons of aviation gas.

Well this time when I arrived at the lodge airstrip with my load of fuel, I discovered that the landing gear indicator read, "that the landing gear did not go down on the left side".

I tried several times to lower it but to no avail. Naturally, I realized that I DID NOT dare to land on the airstrip at Elk Island, with my load of five hundred gallons of fuel, and my aircraft tanks showing half full as well. So I turned around and headed back to Winnipeg.

Now all airplane pilots are trained, that if you are carrying extra fuel, such as in a "bladder," you MUST "dump" the fuel. Well, since I was carrying a "bladder" full of fuel, I told the employee I had with me as a helper, "to stick the drain hose out the freight door and dump the fuel". After about forty-five minutes, I noticed that "droplets" were dripping from the ceiling of the airplane cabin.

Now what had happened was, that there was a draft behind the airplane, and some of the "fuel vapor" droplets, were being "sucked" back into the tail section of the aircraft. I had my employee immediately "shut off" the drain hose and close the door.

So now what do I do? With the fuel dripping from the ceiling, I was an aerial Bomb "waiting to blow"! You see, in the Twin Beech, everything was electric, the landing gear motor, the flap motor, and the radios. I was afraid to shut-off the master switch, because if we had a spark, we would BLOW UP !!!

But I finally shut-off the master power switch and, "Thank God" nothing happened! We flew the rest of the way to Winnipeg without any radios or power. When we reached Selkirk, which is about twenty miles north of Winnipeg, I had to radio the Winnipeg Tower, as we were in their traffic control area, and request permission to land.

Again I knew that when I turned on the master power switch, that it could possibly be the "last thing I would ever do on this earth!" But okay, SWITCH ON. Whew! Nothing Happened! Alright, here we go again, "turn on radios", AND again, Nothing Happened! "Thank God"!!

When I called the "tower", I told them my problem and asked for a "fly over", so the tower people could take a look and see if both my landing gears were down. It was approved, and I flew low and slow three times. The tower told me, "they thought the landing gear on both sides looked like it was down", but I knew that the left landing gear probably was not locked and the landing gear could collapse when I landed.

Then I asked permission to land on the grass next to the runway. I again made a perfect landing on the right wheel, and held the left wheel off the ground until I had lost "flying speed". Then I let the left wheel come down and found that it WAS locked. But the tail wheel had NOT come down, and the "tail fins" were now resting on the grass. But, "Thank God" there was NO major damage AND "Thank God" again, we didn't Blow UP!! I then manually lowered the tail wheel and tied the tail wheel to the "down position" and taxied over to our parking area.

One of the last memorable experiences I will share with you is, when Del and I were doing trade shows for our fuel cell business. You see, Del and I had given the running of the fuel cell business over to our two sons, and we were only doing the trade shows to advertise for the business. We did up to seventeen trade shows a year promoting the business; from Anchorage, Alaska to Hawaii, Canada and the U.S. coast to coast.

Well we had a trade show in Minot, North Dakota in the month of late October, possibly early November; it was winter and a very "nasty cold" day. I told Del that it would be a good idea to take the Aztec because it would be a nice trip and a lot shorter than driving.

The Aztec has a terrific cabin heater (furnace) so I put my parka (heavy coat) in the luggage compartment, Del decided to keep hers as she said she felt a little cold.

We filed a flight plan which is a requisite when crossing the Canada, U.S. border. Upon reaching the U.S. border, the heater in the plane went out. The outside temperature was minus-thirty degrees, so the inside of the cabin instantly became minus-thirty degrees also, and I was wearing a

102

dress shirt. Talk about cold!!

I called Flight Service and cancelled my flight plan and informed Aircraft Control that I had to return to Winnipeg and St. Andrews Airport due to the problem of my airplane heater going out. Okay, More Fun! I then called Winnipeg Traffic Control and was informed that the area was below visual flying rules (VFR) and that I had to fly instrument.

I told them my problem and asked for special permission to fly low, because of ice fog and a very low ceiling (cloud height from the ground), which thank God, I was granted. By this time I was so cold that I felt like I was a "zombie", anyway with our visibility only about one-half mile, I finally was able to locate St. Andrews Airport. I next received permission to land and lowered the aircraft landing gear, and Oh No, what next could happen? The landing gear would not come down!!

Well again I can say, thank God the aircraft had an emergency "hand pump", which I used to lower the gear (wheels) and land. I taxied to our hangar, put the airplane inside and loaded up the Suburban and took off.

We drove all day and night to make it on time to be ready when the trade show opened, but we did make it

Chapter Thirteen

New Horizons Ahead

During the time I was flying for Stevens Point Asphalt Products Company, I would move my family of three small children and my wife to Red Lake, Ontario where we rented a place for the months I flew for the company and then ourselves, flying fishing/hunting charters.

Del and I like the community of Red Lake and decided we would like to live there; we started looking into buying a flying service on Howey Bay.

Holiday Airways came up for sale and we started negotiations to purchase the business. We even looked at property to buy and build our home. Our oldest son, "Butch" was attending kindergarten, and our daughter, Karla was in pre-school. We attended the local Mennonite Brethren Church, making friends and becoming part of the community.

Erich was a little guy at home and Del was expecting our fourth child, I of course was flying everyday unless the weather was too bad to do so.

In the fall of 1968, I got a charter to fly three fishermen up to Gods Lake for a four day fishing trip, this was to be my last trip for that season before we returned to our home in Three Lakes, Wisconsin.

Gods Lake is two-hundred and sixty air miles north of Red Lake, the weather was good, and so off we flew. But being that Gods Lake was actually in northern Manitoba and the month was October, the weather could get a little bit "iffy," and that is what happened. The four day fishing trip actually became a fourteen day trip instead, due to the weather turning very "nasty" and totally un-flyable.

There were no TV's or telephones in the north at that time, only a radio-

Figure 61 & 62: Pictures of "Howey Bay"
in Red Lake, Ontario.

telephone which is a "transmitter/receiver". Let me try and explain what a radio-telephone was. It is a low-frequency "radio" in the shape of a large square box; which has a microphone on the side with a button you would "push" to talk into.

The radio operator, who was in Selkirk would answer, you would "key" the microphone and give the operator your name; the name and phone number of the person you wished to talk to. The operator would "key" her microphone, and ask you to "stand by", which meant for you to wait. She would dial the number that you gave her; tell the person that answered, that they had a radio call, and then tell them to "stand-by". The operator would again "key" the microphone and tell you to go ahead and talk, as your contact was on the line. You then "keyed" your microphone and spoke to the person. When you finished speaking you would say "over," which told the other person that they could then speak.

This took some getting used to, as both people could not talk at once, only one person could speak at a time. The other listened and then could reply. You had to remember that at all times everyone throughout the north was able to hear both sides of the conversation. One of the biggest problems with this was that the radio would only "work" when the weather was good.

Because of this problem, and that I was able to get longer range or distance for my calls from my aircraft radio-telephone, I would go out every day to my airplane and "reel-out" a wire antenna to try and contact an aircraft flying over Red Lake or near Red Lake. Or I would try to contact, Ontario Central Airlines to get a message through to, Del to let her know I was alright and what was happening.

I'm going to take a moment and explain about the "wire antenna". In those days, an airplane was equipped with a small wire that ran over the top of the airplane with a small "wind-sock" attached to the end of a wire antenna. This was attached to the top of the airplane tail, and it could be "reeled" out to about thirty feet behind the airplane. It had a control inside the airplane so that you could wind or "reel" it out and in; then you could transmit or receive on your aircraft radio-telephone.

So every day, I would use my aircraft radio-telephone, and "run" the antenna out behind the airplane, fasten it to a tree, then climb back into the airplane and radio-telephone Ontario Central Airlines. They would call Del for me and relay any message I had for her. Again the biggest problem doing this was, that everyone around could hear what was being said, so you had to be careful. The reason I did not use my regular aircraft radios, was because they are high frequency (the higher you are, the longer the range), and in bad weather, I could not use my regular aircraft radios at all.

Anyway, when I arrived back home in Red Lake, I was really "hopped" up about purchasing a fishing camp on Gods Lake! Del, God bless her, didn't "blink an eyelash", she simply asked, "what about the flying service, Holiday Airways".

I showed her the pictures of a camp on Gods Lake (of course it was not the camp I was talking about) I also told her, that we would have a flying service as I was going into business with a man I met at Gods Lake who had a "bush" airline called Taylor Airways, and I was able to obtain a fifty percent ownership in this small airline.

This way I could legally fly my guests to our outpost camps or fly guests and staff from Winnipeg; I was also able to fly all of our supplies into the camp. When Gilbert Burton was too busy, I could also fly some of his charter flights if I had any spare time.

And, this was the start of something new!

Figure 63: The Howey Bay Motel, where my fishing and hunting guests stayed before and after returning to Red Lake, Ontario

Figure 64: Mitches Grocery Store in Red Lake, where we did our grocery shopping for the family.

Chapter Fourteen

Unchartered Skies and New Challenges

When I, and my family finally arrived back at our home in Three Lakes, Wisconsin that fall. I found that the men I had flown to Gods Lake, and who had wanted to invest in the "deal" with me to buy the fishing camp on Gods Lake called Elk Island Lodge. Had rethought the "deal," and had decided, that since they were in their mid to late seventies, they were too old to get involved in something that would take them into their eighties before it would really start to "pay-off". So they "backed out," and I figured that Elk Island Lodge was a dream lost.

But as luck would have it, a couple of weeks later, a man by the name of George Junkunc who owned American Lock Company, stopped by my hanger and shop to have me do some work on his airplane for him. We started talking about what I had been doing and I told him about flying up to Gods Lake and the fishing camp I would like to purchase.

He had just finished seeing a film called: "Big Country, Big Fish" which just happened to be about the fishing on Gods Lake. By the middle of November, George and I flew up to Winnipeg, Manitoba in my Aztec, to sign the necessary papers to buy Elk Island Lodge on Gods Lake. I then became the half owner in a fishing camp, called Elk Island Lodge.

The next item of business was to get a brochure printed, a booth made and sport shows booked. Also, around this time, I bought a half interest in Taylor Airways out of Gods Lake Narrows and became a partner with Gilbert Burton, a Métis gentleman who owned the "bush" flying service. Between us, we owned several different aircraft including: a Beaver, an Otter, a Cessna 206, and a Cessna172 all of them on floats, and an Aztec and eventually a Twin Beech both on wheels.

Gods Lake does not have any roads into the area, therefore we used floatplanes for both our transportation in and out of the lodge, and for getting food and supplies in. Gilbert and I became good friends and would visit each other several times a year after I sold the camp on Elk Island, and remained good friends until his death.

Figure 65: Del and I in booth for our new venture. God's Lake Elk Island Lodge.

Figure 66: My partner in Taylor Airways Gilbert Burton with his wife Doris, in front of the fireplace at the lodge.

Okay, back to my story, when January 8, 1969 rolled around, I started doing sport shows accompanied by my wife, and three small children. In

February, we took a few days off from doing sport shows, so that Del could give birth to our fourth and youngest child, a girl we named, Colleen. Ten days later, Del, I and now four children (one of them a baby), were back on the job doing sport shows, this time in Milwaukee, Wisconsin. Then in March, I returned to Winnipeg, Manitoba to make arrangements to purchase our first major shipment of supplies. Such as: gas and oil for the boats and airplanes, propane, bedding, paper and cleaning products, our major canned food supplies, flour, sugar, lumber for building, and building supplies. We needed enough supplies to last us through the season at Gods Lake. Also, we needed extra fishing supplies for our guests, fishing rods, reels, fishing line, lures and baits.

I also had to make arrangements to have the supplies delivered to Elk Island Lodge by tractor-train. I'm going to take some time and explain what a tractor-train was. It was a lot of enclosed box cars loaded on to large wooden sleighs which are connected together and pulled by a heavy diesel D-8 Caterpillar tractor that was used to haul very heavy loads of groceries and other supplies to the settlements in the north. At the end of the "train" is a heated caboose where the men (usually four) could sleep, eat and get warm, this "train" was driven only in the winter time over man-made winter roads through frozen muskeg, bush, frozen rivers and lakes. The "trains" never stopping moving, the men would take turns driving the diesel tractors and would simply "hop" off and on as was necessary. Or the person driving would need food or sleep at which time another man would take over driving the "train".

When I had finished making the arrangements I flew over to Red Lake, Ontario to talk to an elderly Swede, I knew by the name of Nels Anderson. He had been a fur trapper in his younger days and knew how to build log cabins. So I hired him to go to Elk Island on Gods Lake and build some log cabins and a lodge for me. One of the larger cabins was being used for the lodge and guests at that time. It, like all of the other cabins, had once been the homes of the wealthier and more influential people who lived on Elk Island when it had been a gold mining town back in the 1940's.

Figure 67 & 68: Pictures of the "Tractor Train" (trucks are now used instead).

I'm going to tell you about the camp I had on Elk Island. First of all the island is twelve miles long and five miles wide across, in the middle of Gods Lake, three hundred and sixty-five air miles north of Winnipeg. It was originally the town of Elk Island back in the 1930's and '40's, it was a gold mining town then and actually had three gold mine shafts until WWII broke out and the cost of getting the gold out of the ground and shipping it to Winnipeg became too costly, it was then shut down. The "town" was later purchased by Barney Lamm and used by him as a special "fly-in" fishing camp for some of his more influential and wealthy guests, he sold the camp to Peter Burton (father of Gilbert). Pete ran the camp for about three years and that is when I came to Gods Lake, at that time the camp could hold about forty guests plus staff and guides.

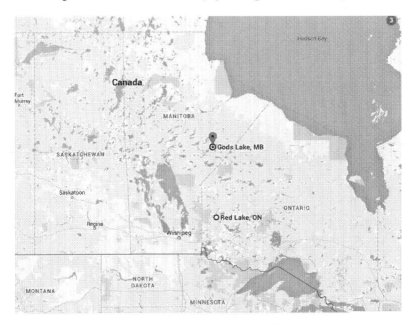

While I was in Winnipeg making arrangements for the supplies, Del remained home in Three Lakes to take care of the children, write letters to the guests and make any guest bookings that came in for the camp during the time I was away. After I arrived back home to Three Lakes, Del, I and the children were again attending sport shows which lasted until about the third week of April.

By May first, I flew back to Winnipeg where I once again checked with Sigurdssons, who operated the "tractor train" carrying our supplies, to make sure everything was going okay and that things would arrive on time. I was concerned, because the weather felt quite warm. But I was assured however, that even though we had the "last train" going out that winter, that there would be no problem getting the supplies to the camp.

After checking with the Sigurdssons, I flew up to Elk Island on Gods Lake to start getting it ready to open for our first guests.

So you know what they say about, "the best laid plans of mice and men"? Well it turned out that 1969 saw an early spring that year and all of the ice went out, the snow melted, the lakes and rivers opened and by May fifteenth the winter roads were closed. All of our supplies got left sitting on the "train" somewhere in the middle of the woods between Selkirk, Manitoba and Gods Lake. Now I want to let you know, that this is approximately two hundred and fifty to three hundred miles of "nothing but trees, rocks, frozen lakes, streams and lots and lots of snow"! Well, that was what it should have been, but now all of snow and frozen lakes and streams were open!!!

Okay, everyone needs a challenge, But DID, I really need one this big? With the "tractor train" getting "thawed down" in the "bush," this meant that I and another pilot by the name of Andy Verrier, that I had hired in Red Lake, would have to fly every day to Thompson, Manitoba (one hundred and eighty air miles away, or to Winnipeg, which was three hundred and sixty-five air miles) in single engine float planes to keep the camp supplied with food and other provisions. Also new beds, bedding and Hudson Bay blankets I had purchased as well as the staff.

Well, Nels at least was getting something done. He finished a cabin and was starting to build our new lodge. When the lodge was finished, it would be forty-eight feet by one hundred and ten feet long and would have a second story on half of it as well as a stone fireplace large enough to burn a six and one half foot log. All of the logs, which were being used, were cut down, peeled and floated to the camp. All of the stones used for the fireplace, also came from the Gods Lake area. This may not seem so very impressive, except you must remember that there were only barges with outboard motors and floatplanes to transport All of the equipment that was used to do this kind of work.

Well the end of May 1969 was fast approaching, I had been flying staff and supplies into camp every day for a month now, and we were getting our first guests around the fifth of June. The cabin I had Nels build for my family was finished and ready to go. It was time to bring my family up to the fishing camp that I had purchased. Del had never seen it, only some pictures of "A" fishing camp, (they were not the pictures of Elk Island Lodge) which I had purchased.

Figure 69: This is what God's Lake looked like in March 1969. I'm trying to get the airplane engine warm enough to start.

I hadn't seen my wife and family since April, our youngest daughter Colleen, was then three months old, besides I could hardly wait to show Del the camp, we had only spoken a few times on the radio-phone and you could not really communicate very well that way. So I flew my Cessna 206 float plane to a float plane base one mile from Selkirk, Manitoba and landed on the river there. I gave Del a call to let her know that I had landed, and drove to the hotel where my family had been staying while I was up north.

Now I wanted to leave right away but of course, Del and Marie Verrier, the wife of my pilot, had a lot of "things" to get ready (I thought they were just "puttering" around) finally they were ready and we headed out to the plane, got everything, and I DO MEAN everything! Loaded up and everybody climbed in.

Figure 70: Del's "new cabin".

By the time we took off it was eight o'clock in the evening and we had at least a three hour flight ahead of us to Gods Lake and the camp. I was going to have to land the plane on the water in the dark, avoid the reefs, taxi up to our dock and tie up. Now I know I had been flying in and out of Gods Lake, back and forth to our camp for a month Hey, "no problem" right?

Figure 71: Al standing on the float of the Cessna 206 getting ready to "tie up" at the dock at Elk Island.

Well, everything went like "clock-work" and we landed around eleven o'clock that night, thanks to some helpful light from the Aurora Borealis lighting our way. I took Del and my family to our new cabin equipped with heat, electricity and running water.

Okay, truth time, the heat was from a wood space heater, a bare light bulb for electricity and the running water was cold, but we were young and together again and our family was with us. I was content and happy, I could now be with my family every day, Del would do the office correspondence, take care of our four children and even greet guests in the evening after they had been out fishing. Why, she was almost on a vacation, Right?

Then "Murphy's Law" came into effect, our cook got a radio-phone call from the U.S., her mother was ill and needed her to come home and take care of her; and since we had a full camp of guests (forty) plus staff and guides, I immediately turned to my wife, after all I was very sure that she could "handle it".

So Del then took on the job of cooking for the camp and guests, as well as the office and prospective guest correspondence, greeting the guests in the evening and taking care of four children. I was busy flying every day just to keep food (the perishables) and supplies in camp, as well as generally running the camp and making sure we had enough guides to go out with our guests.

In the evenings, Del would put our baby daughter on a blanket in the dining room where I could talk to the guests and still keep an eye on Colleen while Del got the food ready for our waitresses to serve our guests.

I have to say, that our baby daughter, Colleen did not lack from attention as all of the guests kept an "eye" on her. Many of the Corporation Presidents and company CEO's would pick her up and hold her. Hey, talk about "High Class" babysitters !

Figure 72: A picture of the original lodge at Elk Island. It held 36-40 guests for a meal. This is where Del started cooking for our guests.

Figure 73: An aerial view of Elk Island Lodge.

Chapter Fifteen

Elk Island and More

The first year we had Elk Island Lodge, the native population used half wild dogs in their dog teams to pull their sleds (this was before they got snowmobiles), the dogs were put on an island out away from the camp and the guides would go about once a week to throw them some fish.

But every so often some of the dogs would make it to the island and then they became a problem. You see the dogs were not afraid of people and they were semi-wild, so you had to be careful when they were around. We always carried "large sticks" or something to protect ourselves with as they would "stalk" you when they were around and because of this, we had to make sure the children were in sight at all times.

Many times in the evenings I would take my family for a walk out to the old number two mine shaft, of course we carried a stick while on our walks, but I was also planning on how and where I could build an airstrip so that we could use airplanes on wheels, which would make it much easier to supply the lodge. That fall, I surveyed out the area that I wanted to use for the airstrip.

By the end of June, I realized that we needed someone to run the small guide store we had. We carried bread, canned fruit, canned pork and beans, Malkin jam, canned milk, pop, snacks, matches and tobacco, as well as fishing equipment and lures for the guests. Eventually we carried everything except fresh vegetables, as the guides and their families would not buy them, we also had clothes for sale.

You see, we were about thirty-five miles from the nearest store at Gods Lake Narrows and had to provide things for our guides and their families that accompanied them. I thought about it and I figured that Del must have a "couple of spare hours" that she could spare to run the store; after all she really wasn't that busy!

By July of 1969, I moved my family to a different cabin, this one was closer to the lodge and the store making it easier for Del to "take care" of both. At this time our daughter Karla, was five years old and she started to help taking care of her baby sister, feeding her a bottle, changing her diaper (they were made of cloth, and you fastened them with safety pins), many times when you picked Colleen up, the diaper would fall off, but it was clean, and Karla even helped to dress her.

Colleen was like a real live doll to "play" with. The two boys, "Butch" and Erich would also help take care of their baby sister, but not as much as Karla.

During that summer, we were informed by some guests who had been at the camp in previous years before we owned it, that they had always had ice cream when they had stayed at Elk Island. Well, since I and one of my employee pilots were flying every day just to keep food and supplies in camp. (to fly ice cream packed in dry ice so it would stay frozen for the one hundred-eighty air miles back) would Not be something I could afford to do, "heck", I couldn't even afford to fly liquid baby formula to camp for our baby daughter, but had to bring in powdered formula instead. As it weighted less and did not have to be kept frozen for the one-hundred and eighty air miles it took to fly back from Thompson.

Well you know what they say about "necessity and the mother of invention"? Well, she did it again, God Bless her! Del once again came through for me. Now I have to tell you, I really do not know exactly what she used or how she made it, but I guess it was some type of frozen "custardy" thing, and she was not able to make a whole lot of it (basically enough for the group that was there) anyway, she told the staff that if any of them so much as even looked at it, she was going to throw them in the lake!

She then made a large pan of baking powder biscuits and took a gallon of strawberry pie filling (no one liked the strawberry pies), thinned the pie filling and served "strawberry shortcake with homemade ice cream" to the guests for their dessert that evening. The guests said it was the best ice cream and strawberry shortcake they had ever tasted. Boy, if they only knew!!

Another time, Del came to the rescue for us. It seems that the waitresses ran out of "thousand island" salad dressing and were "panicking" as the dinner hour was going to start shortly, and all of the guests would be arriving soon.

Del calmly asked them if they had any "Miracle Whip", to which they answered, "Yes". She then asked them if they had ketchup and pickle relish? Again they answered in the affirmative. Del then proceeded to mix the three things together. When she had finished she asked them to give it a taste, they all said, "it tasted like thousand island dressing", and so that solved that "small" problem.

Again the old adage of "necessity being the mother of invention" paid off for us.

Since Elk Island had once been a gold mining town, I took my family on a walk to look around and see the old buildings, gold mine shaft and the old milling plant where they ground the rocks up to get the gold out.

Well that summer, Del and I noticed that our young son "Butch" seemed to always have money. When asked where he had gotten it, he would say, "that the guests had given it to him". We didn't think too much about it at the time and he always shared what he got with his sister and brother by buying them "snacks and pop" from the store.

But just before the camp closed that fall, one of the guests said with a chuckle, "you sure have a great little entrepreneur there", he then proceeded to tell us how "Butch" would give the guests a guided tour of the "old town", the milling plant and other buildings for twenty-five cents a person!

To say that we were shocked would be an understatement! We really didn't know what to do, whether we should praise him or scold him.

Okay, I would imagine that you are wondering how we got the guests to the lodge if we did not have aircraft on wheels.

Well, we used a WWII airplane called a PBY. An amphibian type aircraft which was able to land fully on the water and did not have floats, but the whole bottom of the plane would be in the water.

Then we would use a barge with an outboard motor, to bring it in close to the PBY, and the guides would try to synchronize the barge with the door of the plane so that passengers could disembark. We would then transport the passengers by barge to the dock and then up to their cabins where they would get "settled in".

I have to say, that it was a little unnerving once in a while as you watched the guests getting out of that plane with their luggage, the water under the barge would "raise it up" and the plane seemed to "go down" with the waves. Making it quite a challenge, for our guests, and staff, getting in or out of the airplane and onto the barge.

But the men handling the transfer were good, and they never lost a piece of luggage nor let a guest fall into the water.

Figure 74: A PBY aircraft. This is how we got our guests into Elk Island Lodge the first year.

Chapter Sixteen

Okay, Let's Try This Again

After the last guests left around the middle of September, I flew Del and the children back to Winnipeg, and got them registered in the Winnipeg International Inn Hotel, where they would wait while I returned to our camp on Elk Island. There I organized the native guides to clear all of the brush and trees for our "airstrip". I continued flying supplies into the lodge until freeze-up in late October that year.

I then flew Nels Anderson back to his home in Red Lake, Ontario, in my seaplane. On my return, I flew my plane to the floatplane base in Riverton, Manitoba. Where I had made arrangements to have the floats removed from my plane, and stored in Riverton, (the plane after it was on wheels, I stored at Selkirk for the winter). Riverton, Manitoba is seventy-nine miles north of Winnipeg, a half mile west of Lake Winnipeg, and east of Highway 8.

After, the floats were removed and the wheels back on the airplane, I taxied to the Riverton centre, turned west on Riverton Avenue and taxied one mile through a residential street lined with houses to Highway 8.

(To get the airplane to Selkirk, you had to take off on Highway 8, as there is NO airport in Riverton). My airplane wings were wider than the street, which made this a "little bit" of a challenge. You had to taxi on first one side of the street, and then move to the other side, so you could miss the hydro and telephone poles which were on each side, making sure you did not "hit" any with your wing-tip. If you happened to encounter traffic, you simply waited on the side of the street until the vehicle had passed.

When you finally reached Highway 8, (which was wide enough to take off on), you waited for a "clear" opening and then made a "short field" take off, (this means that you became airborne as soon possible) and then I would fly to Selkirk, Manitoba, where I stored the airplane for the winter.

To be able to do this, the locals would let you know when the RCMP were not in the area (they were only there a couple of days a week), when I got the "all clear", I got my airplane moving. In the spring, we simply did this in reverse. I did this for eight years and never had a complaint or any problem with the RCMP or the residents.

You would not be able to do this type of thing today, because of all the flying laws and regulations.

Then Del drove to Selkirk, picked me up and then loaded our luggage and children into the Aztec, and flew back to Three Lakes, Wisconsin where "Butch" and Karla were enrolled in school, and I started preparing to again do sport shows.

In November of that fall, I flew back to Winnipeg on business. While there, I looked into buying a house for us. It had to be close enough to the Winnipeg International Airport so we could meet guests and make it easy for us to get supplies to the camp. I brought Del and the children up to Winnipeg in December of that year to our new house at fifty-five Lipton Street.

The house was completely bare of any furniture, so we looked through the Winnipeg Free Press newspaper for used furniture, and found an ad, from someone who was moving to the U.S. We bought everything she had, including a Christmas tree, but she only had one bed and the children had to sleep on the floor in sleeping bags that first night, they thought it was a great adventure.

The next day we went and purchased beds and bedding for them and a crib for the baby and prepared to spend Christmas in Winnipeg in our new home. We returned to Three Lakes after the New Year so the children could go back to school.

Andy and I left for Chicago to do our first sport show of the 1970 season. During the winter months of that year, I flew back and forth to

Winnipeg on business several times. On one of the trips I secured a grader and a driver to drive it to Gods Lake and our camp over the winter roads so we could start building the airstrip.

During March, in between doing sport shows, I purchased a big bulldozer for the camp as well as new aluminum boats and motors (we had used Hudson Bay freighter canoes for our first year), these were flown to Tom Ruminski's Gods River airstrip, and as soon as the lake opened up, we put motors on the boats and "drove" them across the lake to our camp. I also made arrangements for food and supplies for Elk Island Lodge, that I would fly up as soon as the ice opened enough to land a floatplane. After the experience we had with the "tractor train", we never again tried using them.

While I am thinking of it, I am going to tell you the story of how we got the big bulldozer to our camp. In the spring, near the end of April, we loaded the bulldozer onto a big Bristol Freighter at Thompson, Manitoba, (this is a large cargo aircraft), and flew it to Tom Ruminski's Gods River Lodge, our neighbor who had a "dirt" airstrip (of course Ruminski's was thirty-five miles across the lake from our camp). When we landed at Ruminski's with the bulldozer, the employee who flew for me, Andy Verrier, was an "old 'dozer" driver, and he agreed to drive the bulldozer the twenty-five miles across the lake to Elk Island.

Bristol with supplies like boats and barrels of gas

As Andy started out driving, the ice started to "break-up" behind him, so he opened it up to top speed and drove as fast as he could to Elk Island where I was anxiously waiting for him. When he finally pulled up on the shore, he was so "shook up" that he actually jumped off the bulldozer and "kissed" the ground, he said, "that when he was driving the 'dozer and the ice was sinking behind him, it felt like he was driving uphill all the way".

Maybe I should mention here, that Gods Lake has depths of over five hundred feet deep, so I was very glad to see that Andy had made it, and I could definitely understand the way he felt!

Then I returned to Three Lakes and brought back a man named, Ed Pafrath. He was a heavy duty equipment operator, and he immediately started right in to bulldozing land for the airstrip.

When Ed started bulldozing (the area was made of gold mine-trailings) over to the boundaries of the proposed airstrip; we discovered there was a large outcropping of solid rock, some of which was fifteen feet high, and it was in the "centre" of the proposed runway, some of the rock even extended to the outside edge.

Now I had heard that the gold mines in Thompson, Manitoba had a strike going on with their "underground miners". I talked to some of the local business suppliers I used in Thompson, and they suggested I should find and talk to some of the men (Diamond Drillers). These are the men who have the experience in drilling holes with the proper spacing, and depth and also "slipping" dynamite sticks into the holes. Running fuses from the dynamite and properly "capping" the holes to blast loose the rock you need separated. This is how they would do it when they were underground and making perfect tunnels and chambers to get at, and remove the gold bearing rock.

I found several of these men who were interested, and made a deal with them. I promised to pay them the regular wage they received from their "gold mine" employer.

Then I rented a large air compressor and two diamond drilling units (they look like a "jack hammer" that you see being used to break up concrete

126

roads and sidewalks). But these "units" have a rod which "hammers" and also rotates or drills.

Okay, one problem solved. Now to get my "crew" to Elk Island, no problem! Next, to fly in the equipment, no problem! Then "problem"!! I had to pick up some fresh diamond drilling rods and twenty cases of dynamite along with reels of fuses and dynamite caps. NOW, it is illegal to fly dynamite, fuses and caps in the same load, BUT, I had to do it! I was very pressed for time to get the airstrip ready for our tourist season.

So I loaded the Aztec and had a "heck" of a heavy load, (of course I had on my mind, was what if I had a "forced landing"), I could become an atomic BOMB!! I then landed at Gods Lake Narrows and had everything transferred onto a barge and "shipped" forty miles by water to Elk Island. (Because a barge was very slow moving, it took six hours to reach the camp).

Well the drilling and the rock removal went great! But then the unexpected! Why is it when everything is going well, there is always something that comes along to "throw a wrench" into it? Alright, back to the story.

One of our guides came and informed me that another guide, named Leslie James, had taken a case of the dynamite and was threatening to "blow up" the lodge and camp if I did not give him a case of "booze". Leslie left instructions for me to leave it in a certain place, so I would not physically be able to get in contact with him.

Now, the nearest RCMP detachment was at Norway House, Manitoba, which was at least an hour or so flight to Gods Lake and our camp.

So I got on the radio-telephone, and by luck, the signals were good and I could get through. I then received their standard answer, "they might be able to send an aircraft by us in several days." My response was, "This was a native man who had stolen a case of dynamite, and he had learned how to use it working with the diamond drilling crew and this was a deadly threat"!! I also told them, "that if they didn't immediately send a plane with RCMP, I was going to shoot the S.O.B. when I found him"!!

Of course, everyone in the north was able to hear this on their radio-telephones, and I immediately heard their response. "Tell 'em Hartwig, tell 'em to move their lazy asses!" I can tell you, that within one and a half hours, a Twin Otter and Beaver landed at Elk Island with a detachment of at least eight RCMP officers.

They went down to the settlement where most of the guides and their families were living. They found at least half of the people drunk from drinking "Bean Juice". This is an alcoholic beverage that the women make out of, dried beans, raisins, sugar, water and yeast. It is totally disgusting! It looks like liquid "Jergen's Lotion", and tastes like stale beer. It has a very high alcohol content, and if not drank within three days, will become very "toxic". The native people become very drunk, sick and belligerent from drinking this.

Anyway, the native women were "spitting" and throwing stones at the RCMP officers, but the officers finally found where Leslie was hiding. He refused of course to tell them where he had hidden the dynamite. So they took him "aside" and "physically" persuaded him, to give them the needed information, (which he then gladly did).

The RCMP arrested him and took him to Thompson, and several days later, he returned after the effects of the "Bean Juice" had worn off. He apologized and admitted that he had been drunk. You see, when the native people get drunk, they do not know what they are doing, and this is what every Court Judge will decide in these kind of matters.

Figure 51 & 52: Our Twin Beech on the Elk
Island Lodge airstrip.

Chapter Seventeen

Once More into the Fray

I again brought Del and the family up to the lodge in May of that year and we enrolled all three of our children, "Butch", Karla and Erich in a "native school" for the months of May, June, September and October until freeze-up. These were all "one-room" school houses and I flew the children forty miles twice a day, both to and from school in a float plane.

Many times, I would have to "scrape" the ice off my floats in early May/June as well as late September, early October, so that neither the children nor I would slip and fall into the icy-cold water.

Actually, that happened one day when I had flown the children to school, I "jumped" out onto the float to catch the dock and stop the plane at the "school", so I could tie it up and the children could get off. I did not realize that more ice had accumulated on my floats from the spray when I had "taken-off" from Elk Island, so when I got out onto the float I slipped and fell into the water.

In fact, I almost went under completely but was able to "grab" both the plane and the dock and get back out of the water and tie-up, so the children could go to school. I then flew back to the camp in very "icy cold wet clothes".

One of the classes that our children were given was English, as all of the native children spoke their native language, which was Cree and they had to learn to speak English. The teacher told us that our three children were very good in this subject, I wonder why? Maybe because that was the language WE spoke do you think?

While our children were attending the "native school" and would go out for recess and during lunch, they had to keep a watch for the wild-dogs that were roaming around.

Figure 53 & 54: Al directing the moving of materials for building.

Remember my telling you about the half wild dogs? Well the dogs were everywhere and every year, one or two children were mauled or killed by these half-wild animals, so when the children were playing outside they always had to be alert. If someone saw one of these "dogs", they would shout "Wild Dog" at the top of their lungs and all of the children would run for the "school" nearest them (there were three one-room school buildings, and the children were divided into them according to age and school year).

Another problem with our three children going to school with the native kids, was "head lice". All of the native children had a problem with them, so every night when I flew the children back to the lodge in my float plane, and they were "greeted" by their mother, she would inspect each of their heads for these "little pests". I am glad to say we never found any!

One evening, we were awakened by a pounding on our door around midnight, or one am in the morning. I got up and went to the door, where one of our native guides was standing. I asked what the problem was and he replied, his wife was very sick and would I come immediately. So I grabbed a coat and a flashlight and followed him to his cabin.

There I found his wife with her face completely "puffed up" and her eyes swollen shut. I also noticed that her head looked like it had been "hit" with something, it looked quite bad! But this was Midnight, and I really couldn't do anything for her at that time. So we had to wait until "first" light, when I loaded her along with her husband and family, into the seaplane and flew them down to the Gods Lake Narrows nursing station.

The nurses checked her over, and then apologized, but said, there really was not anything that they could do for her, because her injury was three days old! All they could do was give her some ointment to put on her head and bandage it for her. It took me a few days but I finally found out what had happened. Apparently, her husband had gotten drunk and had fallen asleep. Later, around midnight, he woke up and wanted something to eat. He tried to wake his wife, who was also sleeping, to get up and make him something to eat.

She refused, he got angry and hit her over the head with a piece of "wood" and "cut" her head open this knocked her out. It wasn't until three days later that he got worried, because now her face and eyes were so badly "swollen", she could not see to cook or take care of him. That's when he came to me for help. Now I know that this can happen in the best of families, but it sure was New to me. Talk about a "Cultural shock"!!

In October of 1970, we immigrated to Canada where we moved into our new home in Winnipeg and immediately enrolled our three children in school at the Laura Secord School which was one street over in back of our house.

Our son "Butch" was eight years old at this time and in grade three, Karla age seven was in grade two and Erich, five years old was in kindergarten. Colleen was just a year old and would not be two until the next February. I set up an office for Del in our new house and from there she would take care of "booking" guests for our lodge and also would be able to easily meet our guests at the airport. (Del saw that fisherman and any supplies I needed, were sent to Elk Island).

I again attended sport shows in the states and would call Del from my hotel room every day with the reservations and contacts that I had made that day. She would write and confirm the reservations I had made, write any letters that were needed to be written to perspective guests. She would also answer any telephone calls that would come in for the lodge.

When I got back to Winnipeg the end of March first part of April, I again purchased supplies as well as hired staff for the camp. When May came, I could start flying the staff and supplies to the lodge, so we would be ready for our first guests, who would be arriving around the first week of June. Usually there would be enough open water around the edge of the lake at that time, so that you get a boat into the water and do a little fishing.

A lot of fisherman liked to be fishing at this time as they thought that the fish were going to be "ravenous" which would make for some good fishing.

By July we had a "rough" partial landing strip on the island and I made the first flight up to our lodge in my Aztec on wheels. By 1971; we had an airstrip that was 4200 feet long, and could now land regular airplanes, even DC-3 aircraft, which now could be used to fly our guests, staff and supplies to Elk Island. This made operating the fishing camp a lot easier to do. I guess I should also tell you, that the entire airstrip is made of "gold mine tailings"! You could say we had a "Gold Plated" airstrip!

Figure 55 & 56: Elk Island Lodge Airstrip with the lodge and cabins.

Picture of the new lodge.

When the three older children were out of school for the summer months, I would take them up to the lodge with me so I could have part of my family, but also to help Del as she then only had to take care of one child and it would make it easier for her to "run" the office an "operation" from Winnipeg, while I was up at Gods Lake.

During this summer, one of the native girls who our children treated as a "big" sister, and who we thought of as we would one of our own, wanted to get married. She asked me if I would "walk" her down the aisle, I immediately agreed and the whole staff started to plan for her reception. We invited her and her husband's families to the lodge where they would have a meal and then a native three-man live band, would play for a dance afterwards.

We let the guests know about these arrangements and Del and the staff decorated the lodge for the reception. They used Styrofoam cups for "bells" and toilet paper was used for the "crepe paper" drapes and bows. It was a very nice wedding, but a little different from one we would have had here. For instance, no one but Del, the children, Marie Verrier, the wife of one of my pilots and her two children attended, and when I paid the minister, he informed me that this was the first time in thirty years that he had ever been paid for performing a wedding.

The dinner was very well attended though, as well as the "dance" afterwards, where everyone would "jig" to western music. Joanie was very thankful to us, for doing this for her, and I must say, that "Yes", even I enjoyed it.

Figure 57, 58, 59 & 60: Pictures of Joanie and Lawrence Okema's wedding at the lodge.

The new lodge that was built by Nels Anderson, was now ready to be used and we could increase our capacity to ninety-six people a day at Elk Island. We also had a "fly-in" outpost camp, a hundred air miles north on Gods River. The outpost camp had come with the lodge when I purchased it, but we had not used it up until now, because we were working to get our main camp in good "working" order first. So now with the camp on Gods River, we were able to offer the guests who would like to try fishing for trophy Brook Trout, a chance to fly to the Gods River outpost camp and try their hand at catching a big one.

We later acquired several more outpost camps : Chataway Lake camp for big Lake Trout in the warm summer months, Bolton Lake camp for large trophy Jackfish (Northern Pike), Edmonton Lake for moose hunting, and Kaskatama on the coast at York Factory, for goose hunting.

All of these "camps" needed float planes for access, except Chataway Lake (you took a boat into that one), and Kaskatama on the coast, you would use a Twin Beech to fly there. These made excellent side trips for our many guests, especially those who stayed for more than two or three days.

Now you might think that all Del and I did was work, but that was not so. When things would get a little quiet (just a few guests) I would take my family fishing. One time I decided to take them up on Gods River to "try" for some nice sized "brookies," when everything was ready, we flew out. We flew about one hundred miles up Gods River, I landed the float plane, got out and tied it up to a tree which was a little ways from the plane.

While I was doing this, Del was helping to get the kids out. I returned and helped her with the rest. Then I took my light-weight rod and a couple of extra lures, and told her to meet me just ahead. I told her that she just had to follow the shoreline. Del agreed, and I left with ALL my fishing gear, which as I said, consisted of a lightweight rod to catch some of those "brookies" and a couple of extra lures.

Del followed with the children. She had tied a rope around each of the older ones, and Colleen the youngest, was just learning to walk, she carried on her hip. Then Del picked up the diaper bag and lunch bag (in case someone got hungry or needed a drink), she "hung" two cameras around her neck, (I might want to take a couple of pictures) some extra film, my big tackle box (in case my line broke or I needed to get a different reel) and several different sized fishing rods (in case the "brookies" weren't biting and I wanted to try for some Whitefish), and proceeded to follow me. When she arrived at the spot where I was fishing, she sat down on a rock to "take a breather," I turned to her just as she sat down and said, "they aren't biting here, and I want to go a little farther up the river". She didn't say a word, but the look she gave me "should have stopped me in my tracks"! Oh well, what can I say, I guess I was a chauvinist!

Figure 61: Al fishing on God's River, the two boys ("Butch" and Erich) by him.

Chapter Eighteen

A Short Lay-Over

Also after the camp would close at freeze-up, around the middle of October, I would head back to Winnipeg where I would remove the floats and put the float plane in storage for the winter. I would then book the sport shows I would be attending, get new literature printed and make sure the booth was in good shape.

When December came around I and Del, would make arrangements with the children's teachers, so we could take the children out of school early, and so they could take school work with them. Then I would fly us to Mazatlan, Mexico for a month.

We would spend the Christmas Holidays and New Years there. When we would arrive and got into our apartment or house, I would find that I was so exhausted from having very little sleep managing the lodge, that I would actually sleep for the first two weeks we were in Mexico.

When we were going down there at that time, tourists had not really "discovered" it as a place to go for holidays like they do today. Instead you would find dirt roads and streets, and the people were quite poor. We even saw a donkey once that had died, left on the edge of the road going into the city.

The local Farmer's Market was where we did most of our grocery shopping. It had reasonably priced fresh vegetables and fruit and was so completely different from anything we had back in Winnipeg, that we enjoyed shopping there. You could .get almost everything there including clothes.

There was an ocean or swimming pool to swim in, a beach to walk on, and a warm sun shining down on you. While back in Winnipeg, they were experiencing snow, ice and cold. Mexico, now that is what I call a real hardship!

Figure 62 & 63: "Christmas" time in Mexico.

By the time we returned to Winnipeg, and the children were back in school on a regular schedule again, I went back to doing sport shows.

Andy Verrier was helping me, he would do some and I would do some, and that way we could cover more places and towns.

In the early 1970's there was a lot of unrest in the U.S., the Vietnam War was going on, and the young college age people were into the "Hippie" movement of drugs, marijuana, PCP, Heroin and others. You know, "burn the bra, burn the flag", "make love not war". The Police were called "Pigs" and were not respected by the younger generation, soldiers who were serving their country were hated and, "spit on," and even called "baby killers", it was not the "best of times".

The Black Panther Party was very active, especially in Chicago, around this time and there were "bombings by the "Weatherman Underground". There were "drive by shootings" at people in their cars, homes were being broken into and people killed and Charles Manson and his group were "busy". Gas shortages were everywhere with long lines of cars waiting and hoping that they could "fill up", before the service stations ran out of gas.

It was not the best time to be in Chicago doing a sport show, but you go where you get people to "book" for your camp.

During the 1972 sport show season while Andy and I were working at the Kansas City Show, I got the Asian Flu which was very prevalent at that time, but I had to continue on to Chicago to the old "Stock Yards Arena", where the Chicago Sport Show was being held. The first day I got there, I was so ill that I could hardly sit on a stool and talk to people.

Since this was a full ten day show, I knew I needed help. So I gave Del a call and asked her to come to Chicago and take over for me.

She immediately made arrangements for someone to take care of our four children, (one of which was a baby), and booked an airline reservation for Chicago that same day.

When she came into the arena I was so glad to see her, as I was almost passing out from my extremely high fever. She took over for me immediately, and I went to lay down in one of the other exhibitor's room, which was located in the Stock Yard Inn Hotel, to wait for her until the show was over that night.

When the show closed that evening, and we arrived back to my room, at the Howard Johnson Hotel in downtown Chicago, which was on Lake Shore Drive. I immediately climbed into bed and can actually say, I was so sick, I do not remember anything after that.

Figure 64: Al and Andy Verrier in booth for Elk Island Lodge.

Anyway, the next day when Del was ready to go to the show, my partner, George Junkunc had one of his men drive her and help with the show.

About Wednesday or Thursday of the following week, I woke up feeling a little bit better and was even hungry, so I asked Del to pick up some cottage cheese or ice cream for me when she returned to our room.

That evening after the show, John, the man who was helping and driving her, drove her to a little "mom and pop" grocery (there weren't any 7-Elevens at that time) to pick up something for me to eat. As she and John got out of the car and started walking towards the store, a Black gentleman pulled up in a Cadillac, rolled down his window and yelled something. Del didn't pay any attention to what the man had said, and just kept on walking towards the store.

John told her to stop, turn around, not to ask any questions, but get back into the car immediately! He said, that they had to get out of there fast or they were going to be in "Big trouble". Del did as she was told and they drove away fast. John told her, that the man had said something about killing them. As they pulled away, the man tried to turn his car around quickly, but instead, he "hit" a hydro pole. Del was slightly "shaken" when she got to our room.

The only other thing that happened, while we were in Chicago during that time, was there had been two robberies in the hotel where we were staying. One happened, on the floor above us and one happened on the floor below us. We were not bothered though, (maybe it was because I was in the room all of the time), which was a good thing. Because I had a lot of deposit money from customers in the room with me!

John continued to help Del with the show, and they didn't have any other incidents after that first one. By the last couple of days I was able to be back on the job with her and we finished the show together, packed up the booth the last day and were ready to head back to Winnipeg.

There was one other thing that happened; actually it was kind of funny. I was craving ice cream, and I saw this restaurant named "Jack Webb" it was in a Black neighborhood. I parked the car and got out, and insisted that Del come with me, although she was very reluctant to do so.

We went in, sat down and I ordered my ice cream. We were the ONLY non-Black people in the restaurant. Now, I don't know who was more nervous, the waitress, Del or the other patrons. But I figured, we were all people and this was a restaurant, and I was going to enjoy my ice cream, after all, I had been sick and I had not been able to eat anything for over a week.!

Figure 65: Al and Del.

Chapter Nineteen

Another Day, Another Dollar

During the 1971 tourist season at the lodge, I realized that when guests were really "getting some action fishing", you never knew where they had gone to catch the fish. Or if one of the boat motors happened to "break down", we had a hard time finding the boat.

We would ask the guides what island a "certain" boat was last seen near, and they could not tell us, as none of the islands had names. The guides were familiar with the seventy or so mile long lake and where generally the fish could be found as they had lived there all of their lives, but that was about it.

So Del and I took a topographical map of Gods Lake and proceeded to name the islands. We gave them our first names, last names, names of our children, relatives and staff, until all of the islands and bays that were not named now had names. I then took the map that fall, to a Government survey office and asked to have it printed.

At the Government office, we were informed that we had to use names of long dead Canadian heroes, instead of the names we had used. But we did not know enough names of dead Canadian heroes at that time, because we were from the U.S., and had just immigrated to Canada. It took a little doing but I got them to print a map for me anyway, which I then had reprinted so I could sell it to our guests and use it myself to know where we were when I was out on the lake.

That was done in 1972 , which is around forty-three years ago. This map is still being used by the three remaining fishing lodges on Gods Lake even today and has been seen and used by hundreds of people so far.

I find it kind of interesting to think that our names and those of our family and relatives and the people who worked at Elk Island Lodge for us will have their names long remembered, even after they are long gone from this earth, and all because of a map. Now that is quite something!

I had all four of our children at the camp with me during the 1973 summer months and the camp was in full swing; we were now holding ninety-six guests per day plus our staff and guides.

Figure 69: A picture of the four kids in a boat.

A typical day for me at this time was: I would be up by five o'clock am in the morning, to check and see how many guides were sober and able to operate a boat and motor safely, (we never allowed any guest to go out onto the lake by themselves), if there weren't enough guides (we needed one guide for each two guests in a boat), sometimes I would have to fly my float plane to the nearest settlement and hire guides and fly them back to the camp by seven o'clock in the morning, as the guests were ready to go fishing by eight o'clock .

Several times I even had to "pull" some of my male staff off their jobs to act as guides, because most of our native guides were "drunk" that day (during the time we owned the camp, we could only use the local native guides, now the lodges in the area can hire out of work fishermen from Nova Scotia and Labrador/Newfoundland). Oh well, that's the way it goes.

I'm going to take a moment here, to tell you about an interesting thing that I saw happen. I had had to fly to Oxford House, a settlement, roughly one-half hour flight west of Gods Lake, anyway I picked up several guides who said that they knew Gods Lake, and brought them back to Elk Island Lodge with me.

Figure 66: A Picture of some of our regular guides taking a break.

Figure 67: A picture of all the fishing boats lined up at the dock.

Figure 68: A "flotilla" coming back to the lodge.

Now it just so happened, that one of the guides I brought back with me, hated one of the other guides that was working for me at the camp; and if they would see each other outside, they would actually fight. Anyway, the guide I flew back, simply walked up to a house, looked inside, saw that there was a space where he could lay down that night, went inside through his bedroll down in the corner, came back outside and went guiding. I thought this was quite amazing. Then I read a book which was a five year thesis study of Gods Lake and the business potential there do to fishing and gold mining.

One of the parts in the book talked about a Reverend Father Leon Levasseur, who was an authority on the Swampy Cree culture (which are the people living in the Gods Lake area) as he had spent most of his life among these people.

He explained the underlying attitudes of these peoples behavior was sharing and feeling. The concept of sharing was a logical response to the native's early environment. The land was huge, game plentiful and time endless. There was no strict division or organization necessary as nature might bring calamities because it was unpredictable and the preparation for this was done by sharing in time of plenty. Reciprocal treatment was expected in time of need.

Leadership was based on the ability to provide, all property was public and everything shared, this included: dwellings, food and other property; because of this they do not view taking something from someone else as stealing like we do.

They believe in putting off doing things until tomorrow, because things might change and then they wouldn't have to do it at all. For instance, they would not cut any wood for the winter as we would do, but instead go out every day and cut down a "green" tree to burn for heat and cooking.

When they started receiving "welfare", they figured that this was normal and the "great White Chief" is the provider and therefore they really deserve to be "taken care of". Of course, this is not the way we were taught, and it is very hard for us to understand this way of thinking; plus, when you are "running" a business and trying to make a living up there with them, and have to "deal" with people who think this way and who are drunk most of the time, not to mention the other problems you have on a daily basis with them; it sort of "colors" your way of thinking.

Now this is not to say that there are not a lot of "good" people among them, because there are and I can count many as friends; but you do not view them the same after my experiences, of which I've only told you a few .

But I have to say, there were very few times that I actually had to use the rest of my male staff to act as guides; because I kept a very close check on this, and if necessary would fly to other communities to get guides.

Okay, back to what I was telling about my typical day. As soon as our guests were on their way fishing, I would fly any guests who were booked to go to an outpost camp for the day. Then after dropping these guests off, I would fly to Thompson or down to Winnipeg for food and supplies. You can imagine how much food and supplies was needed to feed and take care of ninety-six guests, forty-eight guides and twenty-eight staff, we were actually a "small community".

At a couple of the outpost camps, our guests would overnight; these were Bolton Lake Outpost Camp and Gods River Outpost Camp.

Bolton Lake and Gods River outposts held four persons each. When the guests went to these outpost camps, I had to fly food and supplies for both the guests and the guides which would accompany them.

The guests would overnight and I would fly in the next day and pick them up after getting the boats out onto the lake with our lodge guests.

In the evenings, I was back at the lodge waiting for the fisherman to return from their day out on the lake. I would always be in the dining room during dinner time and would "attend bar" from nine o'clock at night until midnight so that I could talk to the guests and hear if any of them had experienced any problems that day.

I usually didn't get to bed until after midnight and at five o'clock am the next morning; I would be ready to do it all over again. This was the pattern of my days while we owned Elk Island Lodge.

GUESTS ARRIVE AT AIRSTRIP

By 1973, we were flying two DC-3s three times a week into Elk Island Lodge with guests and supplies from Winnipeg, every Tuesday, Thursday and Saturday. However, because the DC3s carried all of our guests, they could not fly up much in the way of supplies; which meant that I and another pilot had to still fly to Thompson or Winnipeg daily to keep food and supplies in the camp.

"Butch" and his brother Erich were working as "shore-lunch" boys. This was a job where you packed wooden boxes with food and utensils to be used for a "shore lunch", (the guide would filet, clean and fry fresh caught fish for the guests to eat at noon, but some guests might not like fish). So the box was packed with: lard and margarine for frying the fish, breading for the fish, cans of potatoes, raw onions, bread, lunch meat, canned fruit, Klik (this is a canned meat like Spam), sugar, canned milk, coffee and tea. Included were also, metal plates, cups, eating utensils, a can opener, a sharp knife for slicing onions and potatoes for frying, a frying pan and a coffee pot (to be used over a campfire) AND a garbage bag.

We insisted that the guides bring back All of the empty cans and garbage, if they didn't, we would charge them for it, otherwise, we would have to pay someone extra to go and "clean up" the shore lunch places as the guides were simply used to just throwing the empty cans and garbage into the woods which attracted bugs and other things as well as making the "lunch site dirty" They also had to bring back any unopened cans that they didn't use (we never got any, as all of the cans would be opened).

Around this time, my son "Butch" asked, "if he could show movies at the lodge" At that time, we did not have telephones or television, and we had to have our own "power plant" just to have electricity (down at Gods Lake Narrows, they had a small " caterpillar generator" to provide electricity for that community).

I agreed, and acquired a sixteen millimeter projector. At that time, you could rent first–run movies for a fraction of the cost, if they were to be shown privately, at a fly-in tourist camp or a senior's home.

"Butch" found that the guides enjoyed westerns, like "The Outlaw Josey Wales" or any action movie. He would "run" around and inform all of the guides, staff and guests when he would be showing the movie, date and time. He then, would purchase pop, chips, and chocolate bars at our store and make up tickets.

His "theatre" was the enclosed front porch of the lodge; and he would set up the screen, benches and chairs and his "concession" table and he was open and ready for business. When everyone arrived for the movie, he would sell them a "ticket", snacks and a pop and when everything was ready, he would start the movie.

Now the way the movies were shown then, was you showed one reel at a time. When the first reel was finished, you would rewind it and while it was rewinding, "Butch" would again "open the concession stand". When the first reel was rewound, he put on the last one.

He had to purchase all of the snacks and pop and also rent the movies, any money he had left over from this, went towards buying his clothes for school and anything else he wanted.(He actually made some good money doing this).

Almost every one of our guides, their families and our staff would attend, as well as some of the guests, and when the camp was full, we employed a total of forty-six guides. So I guess you could say, that "Butch" had quite a "booming" business!

Figure 70 & 71: Our outpost camps, Bolton Lake- for trophy Northern Pike and God's River for trophy Brook Trout.

Figure 72: A picture of Al unloading a group of fishermen at one of our outpost camps.

Figure 73 & 74: Gilbert Burton, my partner in Taylor Airways, in front of cabin #8, (Erich is on the back of the truck). Also Gilbert is in a boat by the dock.

Figure 75: Al gassing the Cessna 206

Figure 76: Gilbert helping Al gas the Cessna 206. (Note: the "pail" with the funnel and the "felt" hat strainer.)

Elk Island Lodge Brochure.

Gods Lake Map with Islands Names of Family, Relatives and Staff

Chapter Twenty

More Challenges, But Still Flying

At Gods Lake just like elsewhere, we would get some very "nasty" weather. This one late summer, oh I don't remember, 1973 or 1974, anyway a weather system was coming into the Gods Lake area from the northwest and it was quite late in the evening. The wind had started to pick-up and blow hard enough that it became impossible to turn the float plane so that the front or bow of the floats could point into the wind and waves.

The water from the waves was now slightly "breaking" over the tops of the floats. All seaplane floats have about five separate compartments with bulk heads between them for extra strength, but mostly it was in case of a water leak that only one of the compartments would partially fill with water. Float planes have a "hand" operated float pump that looks like an old fashioned tire pump and the tapered end will fit into the access opening on the top of the floats at every separate compartment.

You usually check each compartment for water leakage or condensation before each flight. The rear of the floats is very small, and the inspection caps on top are only about one foot from the water's surface. The plates are round and about six inches wide.

When waves break over the rear of the float, these inspection caps leak slightly, and have to be pumped out every two or three hours. If you do not do this, the back or rear of the floats will get filled with water and lower about six inches, then the next compartment will start to slowly fill with water, and so on, and so on.

Now I had just hired another float plane pilot who was quite young and did not have a lot of experience, as a "back-up" in case we needed him in

Taylor Airways (my partner, Gilbert Burton operated this part of our business and we had quite a few airplanes in our fleet).

For the first time in my life, I trusted the job of pumping out the floats to someone else! I told this new pilot that he MUST check, and "pump out" the floats every two or three hours during the night. In fact, I reminded him of this several times during that evening. He assured me that he would do this, "no problem"!

Okay? Do you want to guess what happened? No, well anyway, the next morning I went out and found MY seaplane which was tied up at the dock with one float above the water and the other float and wing completely under water!

After questioning this "idiot", he told me that, "yes, he had checked the floats every couple of hours as I had instructed". BUT, "he" DID NOT check the outboard float which, was the only float that would have filled with water (I guess he was too "lazy to crawl" through the airplane and check the other side !).

Figure 77 & 78: Pictures of my Cessna 206 float
plane with a "sunk" float and wing.

I have to tell you, this episode cost Elk Island Lodge dearly!! I had to
hire and fly a scuba diver from Winnipeg (the water was around twenty
feet deep at the dock) who owned a diving school near our home, and
had the expertise in raising an airplane above the water with flotation
gear and equipment.

After the airplane was raised, I had to pump the water out of the floats
and then, ALL of the engine cylinders, magnetos, carburetor and so forth
had to be drained, to get the airplane operational again. Also all of the
radios and navigational instruments were filled with water as well.

Luckily, this incident happened near the end of our tourist season that
year, and I was able to work three to four hours a day on the plane.

With all of the other problems I had "on my plate", this ONE had to top
them ALL !!

Figure 79: Al talk-
ing to guests in
the lounge area
of the lodge.

Figure 80: The dining room at Elk Island Lodge.

Chapter Twenty-One

Okay, Let's Keep Going

That fall, I joined the Masonic Lodge and a few years later became a Shriner. Because of the business, I was not able to become active in the organizations, even though my Grandfather was an active member of the Free Masons and my father was a Past Grand Master of the Masons in Cedarburg, Wisconsin, but I attended whenever possible. I always supported them monetarily and helped wherever I could.

In 1974, Del and I were starting to look for another house. The most important criteria for this was, that it had to be, no more than thirty to thirty-five minutes from the Winnipeg International Airport, so Del could meet our guests arriving in Winnipeg, and it would make it more convenient for sending guests and supplies to camp.

I noticed a house for sale on Henderson Highway, so Del and I went and took a look. We decided we really liked it. The location was perfect for our purpose, and there was an attached garage we could put two large chest-type freezers in, so we could now buy the meat and other frozen food we needed for the camp in bulk. This made it a lot easier for us, because rather than having to buy for each trip, we now had a "back-up" of perishable food and only needed to make large meat and frozen food purchases once a week.

I contacted the phone number that was listed and offered a bid on the house and then forgot about it. I figured that if we were supposed to get the house we would, and if we were not supposed to get it, we wouldn't. Well as "luck" would have it, we got the house, and that fall I moved the family into our new home and we registered the children in Prince Edward School. Colleen, our baby was now five years old and was able to go to kindergarten. Del's office was now in a finished basement, which was a good location for her. In fact we are still living in the same house on Henderson Highway.

I have to tell you how it came that we got our home on Henderson Highway. You see, when I first came to Winnipeg to order supplies for the camp to go up on the "tractor-train". I went into a wholesaler named " McCleans Wholesale"; I placed the entire order and paid cash for it right there. I told the owner, that this should be enough to open an account for me. He said, he never had this happen to him before, and he would not forget me.

We did not know, at the time we put the "bid" in for the house, that the house belonged to Fred Whitely and his wife. Fred Whitely had been the owner of "McCleans Wholesale", that I had "dealt with" way back in the beginning, when I first ordered supplies for the camp. It turned out that they had turned down several other offers for the house, but because he remembered my name, we got it.

Another good thing about the new house was the location, not only was it thirty minutes from the Winnipeg International Airport, but the back yard overlooked the Red River, which meant that I could now fly my float plane directly to my house and "tie" the float plane up at out dock down at the river.

We were now using Ilford-Riverton Airways DC-3s (these are WWII aircraft which hold twenty-one to twenty-four passengers and their luggage) to fly our guests to the lodge. These flights, as I mentioned before, were every Tuesday, Thursday and Saturday, and sometimes we had as many as two or three aircraft flying up on those days. I then decided to purchase a thirty foot moving van, where canned goods and pop could be stored to add to the planes if they were not loaded with passengers. This way, we were getting supplies and also full value for the cost of the flights.

The van was parked at the Winnipeg International Airport at Flyways Esso, which I kept filled. So whenever I flew my six passenger Aztec to Winnipeg I could "top" off my load and fly back to the camp with a load of supplies.

Around this same time, I purchased an eleven passenger Twin Beech aircraft with an aluminum interior and a cargo door. The seats could be removed easily to "ship cargo" or we could use it to transport smaller

Figure 81: A picture of my brother Max in our guide store.

Figure 82, 83 & 84: Pictures of some of the fish that were caught. Al is seen with a guest and a rack of fish, a nice days catch also is displayed on the dock. Our guide foreman, Ted Murdock and one of the guides, hold a couple of huge trophy Northerns.

Figure 85: A load of guests and mattresses in a DC-3 airplane.

Figure 86: Andy Verrier and Joe Amodio, two of our pilots sitting on the float of the Cessna 206, which has just been put back on floats.

Figure 88: Al taking a break from working on the Cessna 206.

groups of fisherman to the lodge. With the addition of the Twin Beech, it now made it much easier to get food and supplies flown to the lodge on a daily basis, especially if something was needed in a hurry. After a couple of years, I hired Joe Amodio, a pilot I knew from Red Lake, Ontario when I was flying there. Joe had just recently moved to Winnipeg, knew how to fly a Twin Beech and needed a job.

I'm going to tell you about a problem I had with the Twin Beech . The plane started using a lot of oil. The cylinders, pistons and rings had to be replaced. I checked out the cost of having the cylinders done in Winnipeg at Standard Aero and was told, they would cost six hundred dollars apiece, for one rebuilt cylinder (this did not include the pistons, rings or piston pins) and I needed eighteen of them.

So I looked around and found a man who used to sell Beech parts for the U.S. Government. He retired, bought up all of the government surplus Beech parts, and went into business for himself selling parts. I purchased eighteen new cylinders with pistons and rings for forty-nine dollars each. This meant, I could now afford to replace the wing tips, self adjusting brakes and also replace the tail wheel. The total cost for all of this was just "shy" of five thousand dollars.

Dean Stickle, my mechanic, I and our four children took off in the Twin Beech, and flew to Van Nuys, California, so we could replace all of the cylinders on the airplane (Del stayed home and took care of the business). Along the way, we had to make frequent stops to add oil from the fifty gallon drum of oil, I brought with us.

When we reached Van Nuys the haze was so bad, that to see the airport you had to be directly over the top of it (you could see less than a mile). This airport did not have instrument approach facilities, so I used my "bush" flying skills to land. Upon landing, we found we had one hundred degree temperature, and one hundred percent humidity! The haze was so thick that it actually burned our eyes.

I found a hangar with no walls, only a "roof," to keep the sun off the aircraft, so we would have a place to work, and parked the Twin Beech. After awhile, I decided that instead of MY doing the work on the airplane, (as I usually did) I would just hire a mechanic to help Dean and then I could take the four kids sightseeing, maybe to Disneyland. Which is what I did, we would go from air conditioned motel, to an air conditioned rental car and to as many air conditioned "tourist sites" as I could find.

It was so hot in Van Nuys, that the mechanics actually kept their tools in a large pail of cold water, which they kept that way, by using a hose to keep the water running and the excess was allowed to spill over onto the pavement. This kept the tools and work site a little cooler and easier to work in.

Figure 87: The Twin Beech airplane in Van Nuys, California. Dean Stickle, our mechanic is standing by the post taking a lunch break.

Chapter Twenty-Two

Onward and Upward

The summer of 1974, I finally agreed to allow my son, "Butch" to take a boat and motor out with guests. I had taught him how to operate a boat, and he had seen how we made a shore-lunch camp and filleted fish. And he had been "bugging me" to allow him to start guiding. I had kept saying, "no" as I felt he was too young, and let's get honest here, Gods Lake is a VERY Big lake. However, the day came and I did not have enough guides, and every one of my male staff had been "pressed" into serving as a guide. But I was still short one, so I finally reluctantly agreed, and that as they say, was "history".

He was so good that a lot of our guests would ask for him. "Butch" was very friendly and knowledgeable about the lake and did an excellent job of guiding for the guests. He actually became one of our best guides. I had to be very careful letting him do this, as I didn't want to insult our native guides.

Also, just for the record all of our children worked at the lodge. Karla, was a "cabin girl", and helped to clean the cabins when she was ten years old. By the time she was twelve, she was "busing" in the dining room and she did this until she was going on fifteen years of age.

Erich started as "grounds keeper" picking up garbage around the lodge and cabins. When he got older, he took over "Butch's" job, as "shore lunch" boy (packing the wooden shore lunch boxes) and packing the frozen fish for the guests to take home.

Figure 89: Karla taking a break from her duties to bring a cake for her Mom's birthday.

Figure 90: Erich driving a boat.

TYPICAL SHORE LUNCH, OUTDOORS AT ITS BEST

The guides cleaned and filleted the fish and brought the fish to the lodge where they had to be wrapped in "butcher paper" and marked with each guests name, (both Erich and "Butch" did this). Erich also helped with the boats. Putting the paddles, life jackets and fishing nets into the boats and then putting them away after the fisherman returned in the evening.

Figure 91: Butch cleaning out the Twin Beech.

The fish were frozen and packed in a styro-foam cooler, for each guest to take home, and no one ever had a problem getting their limit of fish.

As I have said before, there were always problems "popping up" when you run a "bush" fishing camp. First of all, your staff only wanted to work for a couple of months out of the year (our season ran from about May fifteenth to around September fifteenth) and most of them had an alcohol problem. Also about ninety percent of our guides would work for a party just for the length of the guest's stay, (which was three to seven days), and then they would "take off" as soon as they were paid and go on a "drunk". (the going price at that time for "boot legged" liquor, was one hundred dollars for a twenty-four ounce bottle). "Boot-leggers" got this price because Gods Lake and Gods River reserves were "dry reserves" (which means that no liquor was allowed on them).

Okay, one of these problems happened on this particular day. Now I had always told the staff to let me know if we were running short of anything at least two weeks in advance, so that I could plan trips (the closest town was one hundred and eighty air miles away, and Winnipeg was three hundred sixty-five air miles away). Well this day had started out "bad" and looked like it was going to go "down-hill fast" from there.

First of all, I found that most of our guides were drunk and I had to fly at dawn to Gods Lake Narrows to hire more guides and have them back at the lodge before the guests got up and were ready to go fishing. (As I said before, we never allowed any of our guests to go out on the lake without a guide). Next, I was informed that one of the waitresses was stealing and she was causing problems among the female staff. Also the guests were making "jokes" about her and "her bag full of coins from going from cabin to cabin." Then to top this all off, I was told that we were out of toilet paper !!

You have to remember that our camp held ninety-six guests per day, which required forty-eights guides plus our camp staff of around twenty-eight (which included the cook, cook's helpers, waitresses, cabin cleaning staff, laundry staff, mechanics, airport maintenance staff, shore lunch box personnel, grounds keepers, camp store employees) just to name a few, we actually were a small community all by itself. So with at least one hundred seventy-two people using the "facilities", being out of toilet paper constituted a complete emergency!!

To make this even worse, this happened on a Sunday! And all of the wholesalers in Thompson were closed, (they were only open Monday to Friday). Okay, first of all, I got hold of the woman who was stealing and causing the problems, and I fired her on the spot! I told her to get packed in ten minutes as I was taking her to Thompson. I guess, I was a "little angry" by this time.

We took off, and as I was approaching the Thompson Airport, I called the tower and asked them to have the RCMP waiting for me when I landed.

When we arrived, they immediately checked all of her luggage and found, a bag of money, some Hudson Bay blankets, bed linens, a couple of pillows and even a couple rolls of toilet paper! The RCMP wanted me to swear out a warrant for her arrest for stealing, but I said, I just wanted her gone, And I was able to get my stolen items back. I do not know what happened to her, but I guess she made her way back to Winnipeg.

Anyway, I then made at least a half dozen phone calls, and was finally able to get a wholesaler to open and sell a load of toilet paper to me, for a little "extra inducement". I bought enough toilet paper to last us until the following year! I also filled ten empty propane tanks that I had taken along which "topped" off my load.

As I was returning to Gods Lake, I spotted a boat covered with a tarp hiding supplies (guides do not cover anything in a boat with a tarp), and the boat was only five miles south of Elk Island. It was also "riding very low" in the water. So I made a "low pass" over the boat; and knew immediately that they had a "load of bootlegged booze" on board, which made the boat very heavy in the water.

I immediately turned the airplane around, and this time I flew at them at about five feet above the water. Both of the men jumped out of the boat as I reached them. Turning the plane around, I saw one of the men swim to shore, but the other man had gotten back into the boat and was going at "full speed" back south. Turning around again, I flew at him to give him a "very low level buzz", but saw that the boat was turned upside down in the water before I reached him.

Several days later, I found out that the "bootlegger" had hit a reef and ripped the bottom of his motor off and had lost his entire load of liquor. I am not going to say that I am sorry for what I did, as he would have brought it to the camp, sold it to our staff and guides, which would have caused me even more problems.

That evening, I got my whole staff together and told them, that if I had any more incidents like the "toilet paper" fiasco, that there would be some very "severe" consequents that they wouldn't like, and there had better be at least a two week supply of "anything" we used or needed for the camp!

I guess, that little bit of "chewing out" did the trick as we never had any more "last minute" shortages of supplies.

That September, when I brought the children back to Winnipeg so they could go to school, (I had to return to camp, as we had one last big group of men coming that year around the fifteenth of September). Charlie Stortz, and the Pioneer Hi-Bred Company were very good customers, and Charlie insisted that Del be there when his group arrived. We had to get someone to stay with the children so that she could come up. One of the women that cooked for us, Kay Monkman, was leaving camp a little earlier than everyone else, and agreed to stay with the children until Del got home. After the group left, I was going to close up the camp for the season, and since it was only going to be a few extra days, Del agreed to stay behind and wait for me, after all, Kay was with the children, so Del knew that they were alright.

Everything seemed to be going fine. "Butch" our oldest, would call us every afternoon on the radio-phone (Kay was afraid to use it) and talk to Del.

Friday of that week came, and we got the radio-phone call as usual, everything was still good in Winnipeg. Then Monday morning came, and "Butch" again called, this time it was early in the morning, to ask if he or Karla should stay home "again" to take care of their "baby" sister, who was only five at the time, Del asked why they should have to stay home to take care of Colleen, because "Auntie" Kay was there. "Butch" told Del, "that "Auntie" Kay left Wednesday morning and hadn't returned yet". The three older children, "Butch" twelve, Karla eleven and Erich nine, had been taking turns staying home and taking care of their little sister since Kay had left.

To say that Del "freaked out" would be an understatement! She left that afternoon with Joe in the Twin Beech. I remained at camp to close-up.

On approaching the north end of Lake Winnipeg, the ceiling was quite low and there was fog which made the visibility very poor. Joe Amodio who was flying, was afraid to try and make it to the nearest airport. He decided, instead to land the Twin Beech in a farmer's field. The landing was fine, but the plane's wheels sunk to the axles in the mud.

Del and a few of the other staff, who had flown out at the same time, had to walk through the mud up to their "calves", to the nearest highway (which was about four to five city blocks away). There they got a ride to the nearest farm house, and were able to make arrangements to get back to Winnipeg, which was two hours away.

When Del got home, she called me on the radio-telephone and told me what had happened, and I can tell you, she was NOT PLEASED with Joe. She said, "if it would have been me flying, we would have landed at the Gimli Airport, just ten or fifteen minutes more by plane from the farmer's field, which had a nice long paved runway, and was only one hour from Winnipeg.

After I got home, I then made arrangements with the farmer who owned the field, to use his tractor to "gently" pull the plane to the highway, where I was then able to fly to Winnipeg.

Figure 92: Al and Del going fishing to God's River.

Figure 96: A view of the lodge from the boat dock.

Chapter Twenty-Three

Still Hanging in There

As I mentioned before, in the fall of the year around freeze-up we closed the camp, which meant, that everything was put away for the winter. The Hudson Bay blankets and bedding had to have moth balls put among them to keep mice away. Any dry goods were stored in airtight containers and all of the boats stacked up, and any leftover fish or meat had to be flown to Winnipeg along with any other perishables. Some of which was chicken gizzards and hearts, and I do have to say, that Del had to become very "creative" with some of this, when making meals. Also, because we owned a fishing camp in the north, we were allowed to hunt two moose each year, which I would do.

One time in late September before I brought the children and Del back to Winnipeg, we flew up to our Gods River outpost camp to close it up and winterize everything. I told the children, that I was going to "call" a moose that evening before we "turned" in. I told them that the next morning there would be a moose out in front of the cabin. Del and the children got a "good laugh" hearing me "call" the moose. I used a card board roll from a paper towel and made a "loud grunting sound" a couple of times and then went to bed.

Early the next morning I got up, looked out the window, and just as I had predicted, there was a "big Bull moose"! So I "grabbed" my gun and dressed only in my "long johns" ran outside and shot the moose. I then cut it up and loaded it onto the floats and flew it back to Elk Island. Where I had some of the guides help me finish skinning and cutting up the meat.

By 1975 "Butch" was guiding more and more and seemed too really like it, he was now thirteen, Karla was twelve, Erich was ten and Colleen our "baby" was the grand old age of six. Each of the older children were working each summer at the lodge and Del was still "holding down the fort" in Winnipeg", taking guest reservations, greeting the guests at the Winnipeg International Airport and shipping supplies up to the lodge when I needed them.

We purchased an old school bus which we used to transport our guests and their luggage from the International Inn Hotel to Ilford-Riverton Airways where they would board the plane to Elk Island.

In the summer months of July and sometimes August, Del would be able to come up to the camp for a week. During this time, I would have her help me "keep the peace" with the native guides.

You see, the guides would get hold of alcohol and would become very drunk. When this happened, they would start swearing and want to fight, if this happened while Del was at the camp, I would have her go out and "talk" to them and the problem would be defused, as she could usually get them to go and "sleep-it off"; this was the perfect solution to a "nasty" problem, and I would not have to get violent with them.

As I mentioned before, when our guests arrived at the lodge, I would have any guest who had not been to the camp before have a seat. I would then proceed to tell them that "the number one rule" I had, and (IT WAS ETCHED IN STONE!!) And it applied to EVERYONE, was, "NO ALCOHOL TO ANY GUIDE OR STAFF MEMBER"! Now this was for their protection as well as everyone else's. In fact the "rule included", that if they did give any alcohol, to any staff member or guide, they would be put on the next flight back to Winnipeg!

Here is just one incident that happened (and there were a lot more because of alcohol). Well, it was after midnight (it seemed that all the "bad" things, happened after midnight), anyway, one of our guides, came running up to the lodge and "pounded" on the door, which I always locked for the night.

Shouting for help, (now I slept on the second floor of the lodge, which was over the dining room and kitchen). I got up, dressed and went down and opened the door. There stood Lawrence, one of my best guides, he told me that Leslie James a cousin of the James brothers , had just fired off a shot gun, (yes, Leslie James is the same one who had gotten hold of the dynamite when we were building the airstrip) was drunk and had shot someone. Lawrence wanted me to come immediately.

I know that this will not sound politically correct or even nice, but at that time of the night, with one of the guides drunk and shooting off a gun, a person would have to be "crazy" to go anywhere near them, Besides that, there wasn't much I could do as it was too dark to fly any place.

So I told him that I would be down to the guide's living quarters at first light. The next morning, as soon as it was just getting "light", I and Ted Murdock (the guide foreman) went down to Demas's place, and found Demas James lying on a mattress soaked in blood with his foot wrapped tight. We carried him on the mattress to the Twin Beech so as not to do anymore damage and flew him to the nursing station. There they medivaced him to Winnipeg.

I and Ted flew back to the lodge and I called the RCMP. I told them about the shooting, and they came, located Leslie, the cousin to Demas, and arrested him. Then they flew him, his gun and ammunition to Winnipeg. He (Leslie) was back within two days carrying his gun and ammunition!!

The judge in Winnipeg said, "that any native person who is drunk, is not responsible for what he does".

I asked the guides how this had happened. They told me that Leslie had gotten hold of a bottle of rye liquor and had hidden it. Demas (Leslie's cousin) had been drinking the home made brew that they make called "Bean Juice" and was drunk from it. On this particular night, when Demas fell asleep, he fell with his head at the foot of the bed, his feet at the top of the bed, and he was covered up with a blanket.

Steven James, another one of the James brothers, had "sneakly" stolen his cousin Leslie's liquor and had gone off to hide and drink it. When Leslie came home to get his bottle of liquor, he couldn't find it. Then seeing Demas drunk and sleeping, Leslie figured that Demas had stolen his bottle and drank it. Leslie then got mad, grabbed his shot-gun and shot where he thought Demas's head was, but he shot Demas's foot instead. Thank goodness! This was why my "rule" on liquor.

Here is another but different story. This one is about a group of guests that we had around the end of June, first of July that year. It involves a group of six men, who booked a trip to the camp one night with Del, and flew up to the lodge the next day in their own private airplane.

I was very surprised when they landed and I saw six men get out of the plane wearing three piece silk suits and fancy shoes. (I also noticed the gun holsters with pistols they were wearing under their suit coats). They had no luggage at all with them. So they had to go to our "store" and proceeded to "buy everything brand-new"; this included clothes, as well as the best fishing equipment we had, (rods, reels and lures, that type of thing).

I had three of our white male staff act as guides for them. The staff that was guiding them would, report back to me at night. They told me, that they didn't think the men had ever fished before in their lives. As they didn't know how to even put the rod and reel together. Or how to "string" the line or attach a lure, as for knowing how to "cast" or "reel in", that was almost non-existent to say the least! I heard many stories about them "casting" and the fishing rod "flying" out into the water, or about the fishing line getting "caught" up in a tree when they cast. And then the one where the rod got "jerked" out of their hands, are just a few examples of their fishing "skills".

A day or so later, I overheard them speaking "rude and filthy" to some of the waitresses. The waitresses came and complained to me about it. So I went over to the men and told them, if they didn't stop with the "bad" behavior, they would have to leave. After that, there was no more "bad" language or behavior. I had a "funny" suspicion after seeing the guns under their suit coats when they arrived, the way they were dressed, (no luggage and their language, AND they being from Chicago, Illinois), that they might be part of the "Mob" and something "bad" had happened down there. So they had come up to Elk Island Lodge to be "on the lamb" so to speak? (I was afraid to turn them in to the RCMP, in case "I" would end up on a "hit list", when next I did a sport show in Chicago for doing so, and I had to go to Chicago that winter!

The end of September, I again took the family up to God's River outpost camp to get our yearly moose. This year, however, it was "Butch" who got the moose instead of me. It was a "large Bull", and all of the kids got a chance to see it. Then the boys even helped me "clean" it.

We should have registered it that year with the 'Manitoba Big Game Awards', as it would have taken the "top" trophy award for the largest moose shot that year. But we waited one extra year to register it as we didn't think it was actually that large, but the "rack" still came in second, the year we actually registered it.

Figure 93, 94 & 95:
The "family" moose
hunt at God's River
outpost camp.
"Butch" shot this one.

Chapter Twenty-Four

Outpost Camps

Also the year that "Butch" was thirteen and a half, I was having problems having a guide stay at the Gods River Outpost camp, so "Butch" said that he would like to give it a try. I flew him up there along with food and supplies. I then would fly a group of two to four men to the outpost camp in the morning and pick them up the next morning when I brought in a new group. If there were no fishermen to go up, "Butch" would be "on his own". He seemed to "thrive" doing this, and told me of the many adventures he had while being by himself. For instance, this is one of the experiences he told me about. It was when he had gone for a hike and had taken his fishing rod with him to try and get a couple of "broo-kies". Well on the way, he came "face to face" with a timber wolf. He said, He looked at the wolf and the wolf looked back at him, then they both turned around and headed back the way each had come. "Butch" said, it was a little scary at the time, but also kind of funny.

After the camp closed for the season, and I had flown my float plane to Riverton, put the plane and floats in storage for the winter. I then returned to the lodge and flew the Aztec back to Winnipeg. That was when I had a chance to catch up on things. In December, I again flew the family down to Mexico in the Twin Beech where we would spend Christmas and New Years and I could get a chance to rest up before I started doing the sport shows in January.

The 1976 camp season of course opened with a "bang". Our first guests arrived the first week of June and we were under way with a full camp. I had hired a man by the name of Ken (Jolly) Reckinger to help with the advertising and at the lodge. Karla and Erich were back at the camp working the end of June and "Butch" was back up at Gods River, Colleen of course was a little girl and managed to find something to keep herself busy. Her job was to help keep our living quarters tidy. Del was again busy in Winnipeg and Joe Amodio was busy flying the Twin Beech to Elk Island with supplies every day. I of course was busy flying guests out to outpost camps, getting guides when needed, and generally "running" the camp.

When Del was able to fly to the lodge for a vacation, I flew her and the other children up to Gods River, where "Butch" was staying and taking care of the guests who went there to fish for Brook Trout. Del and the family stayed there for a week; and I would join them for a day here and there when I could.

Figure 97, 98, 99: Del and the kids up at God's
River Outpost camp.

From what they told me, I could tell, they had a really "Great Time". Del
even told me about "chasing" a grey squirrel that was "stealing" toilet
paper! They also talked about a picnic they had across the river (the river
was low that year), they said they made "Klik Dicks", whatever that is? I
wish I could have been with them more enjoying all of their adventures,
but I had a fishing camp to run, the guides and staff to deal with instead.
Oh well, I guess that is the way things go.

In late August, before the children went back home, I flew Del and
"Butch" (who was now fourteen years old) to the Kaskatama Goose
hunting camp on Hudson Bay. We took all of the seats out, except the
one extra seat for Del. "Butch" was sitting up front with me in the
"cock-pit" of the Twin Beech. I also made-up beds in the back for us to
sleep on, and a small camp stove in the tail area of the plane. We
"grilled" steaks and potatoes outside the night we landed. We also enjoyed salad and dressing as well as coffee, tea and pop to drink. A propane outdoor light, a pail of ice for drinks, and we had all the comforts of
home! We had our guns and ammunition for goose hunting and were

hoping on getting a few geese to bring back.

Well, we took off a little late from the camp that day and had to fly north westward towards Churchill, because the weather was getting bad and the "ceiling" was getting lower. Once we got up near Churchill we started heading back eastward again, but got so "caught-up" in watching the flocks of geese (Blues, Snow Geese and Canadians) flying overhead in large flocks, that I forgot to keep track of our location, (there was no GPS at that time).

The sky was getting dark and I started looking for land-marks so that I could find the small esker (a strip of sand bar we were going to land on) when I spotted a "strobe-light" from another aircraft (this plane had taken off just before we had). I then flew towards this light and found the esker I was looking for. After we landed, and taxied to our spot, I asked Del to go to the door of the Twin Beech and "thank" the pilot for putting his "strobe-light" on for me.

When she opened the door, the pilot took one look at her and said, "OH MY GOSH, YOU' RE A WOMAN"!! The reason this was said, was she "actually WAS" the only woman there! Everyone else, were men and a "person" could see for miles with only a few bushes here and there.

Figure 100: Our goose hunting trip. Del cooking dinner outside the Twin Beech.

Anyway the next day, I had "Butch" and Del help me carry a tail section from a Cessna 206 aircraft that had crashed, over to the Twin Beech before we started our goose hunting. (You know, work first, play later?)

The Cessna 206 aircraft we had, was one of the first of those models built. The newer Cessna 206's had a larger tail section which was much more efficient, and that was what this one was. So we removed it from the wrecked aircraft on the esker and moved it over to the Twin Beech aircraft until we were ready to leave. The reason we did not put it into the airplane right away, was because the tail section we picked up was about twelve feet long and five feet wide and we had to figure out how to load it into the airplane and still have enough room for the three of us to return to Elk Island.

Now I had given Del a new over-under Berretta shot gun to hunt with. I told her how to load it and fire it. "Butch" was shooting at the geese over head, so I figured she would be okay and I went off on my own to try and get a few geese. Pretty soon, I heard Del fire her gun, and then I heard her fire it a second time. Well, wouldn't you just know it! A goose

Figure 101: Del's goose.

fell from the sky. I was very impressed, as neither "Butch" nor I had gotten anything that day.

Del later told me, "that shooting the goose was a complete accident, as she was JUST trying to get the gun back on safety after firing the first time. But she could not remember what I had told her to do to put the gun back on safety, so she simply fired off the other barrel and hit the "goose" by accident! I still do not know who was more surprised, Del, the goose or me.

The next day, was real nasty, there were very high winds, sleet, and wet snow, "Butch" and I "braved" the weather again to hunt. While we were out hunting, Del stayed inside the airplane with the small camp stove on and hot coffee ready for "Butch" and I when we to came in to warm up. She told me, that all that day, the hunters would "stop by" to see how she was doing. Del said, she could see they were shivering so would invite them in to get warm and have a cup of coffee. She told me, that she had gotten her goose, and didn't need to go out in the "bad" weather to hunt for anymore! The next day we headed back with our geese and I then flew my family back to Winnipeg with our "prizes".

I would have liked to take Erich with us, but he was only eleven at the time and would have to wait until he was a little older to go hunting with me. He finally got his chance to go goose hunting up at Kaskatama (Hudson Bay) in 1980 when he was fifteen. I flew Erich, "Butch", my brother-in-law Mel Oelrich (their uncle) and their Grandfather Roy Oelrich there on a goose hunting trip. It was a very "special trip" as it was the last hunting trip the two boys were able to go on with their uncle and grandfather.

That fall, when closing up the Gods River Outpost camp, upon landing, I spotted two moose. So I taxied up to the shore, tied up the plane, grabbed my rifle and shot both of them, (we were allowed two moose because we had the camp). I put on my rain suit and quickly cleaned them. And because it was starting to get dark and the weather was getting bad, I grabbed the chain-saw and quartered them. Quickly lined the inside of the Cessna 206 with plastic and loaded the moose quarters. I then finished empting the outpost camp of all the perishables, tied the canoe onto one of the floats and took off.

The load was so heavy that I could only fly about three or four hundred feet high all the way back to the lodge. When I pulled up to the dock at Elk Island, the backs of my floats went under water a "little bit". I guess you could say that I was a little bit over loaded?

The year 1977 arrived with us having the largest fly-in fishing camp in Canada, and the largest all log-cabin lodge in the north. The other large camps at that time were Great Bear and Great Slave which held fifty guests each day. We held, as I have said before, ninety-six guests a day. Elk Island had such an excellent reputation when we owned it, that we would even receive requests from people from Thompson and Winnipeg, asking to fly up to our camp to have "dinner and spend the weekend" with us as a "holiday".

I sold my share of the fishing camp to my partner, George Junkunc the fall of 1977, after a very busy fishing and hunting season. I had over heard some of the native men and boys talking and showing an interest in our daughters. I felt it that it would be a good idea in getting them back to Winnipeg. As the girls were becoming teenagers and would soon start being interested in boys and dating.

By the way, when I sold Elk Island Lodge and my interest in Taylor air-ways, I decided that since I was no longer flying commercially anymore, I did not have to keep a "log" of every hour I flew, (which is required when flying commercially).

As of October 1977, my flight hours were:

14,348   Total flight hours

5,700   Float time hours

1,685   Instrument flight time hours

1,425   Flight Instruction hours

I also was a FAA-(Federal Aviation Agency) Flight Examiner, I gave the licenses for:

Private Pilot

Commercial Pilot

Instrument Pilot

Seaplane Pilot

Figure 102: Al in the cockpit of the Aztec.

That fall, after closing the camp, we held a large party for our staff at the Shanghai Restaurant in China Town in Winnipeg. The agreement with the restaurant was, we would supply all of the fish (Lake Trout, Jacks (Northern Pike) and Pickerel, (Walleyes), as well as moose meat), and the Shanghai cooks would prepare and serve it. We paid a fixed price for the entire group. (There was even enough left over, that the Shanghai employees could also enjoy the food).

While I was attending this "farewell" dinner, I was approached by a gentleman who said, He had over-heard us talking, and would be interested in hiring someone like me, and asked that I get in contact with him. A couple of weeks later I did, he then hired me to be a property manager to take care of four hundred and fifty houses at the CF Base on Whytewold Road and Ness Avenue in Winnipeg. I would be working for Metropolitan Properties Ltd., which owned the houses and leased them to the Canadian Forces. I ended up working for them for twenty years.

Figure 103: Our "Farewell Dinner" for our staff.

Chapter Twenty-Five

Let's Try Something New

During the time I worked for Metropolitan Properties, I hired "Butch", Karla, Erich and eventually also Colleen to paint houses for me during the summer. I also helped a man named Emery (Jim) Gurski (he was doing odd jobs and cutting grass) to start a lawn care service at the base. He turned it into a very successful business known now as "Jim's Lawn Care".

Matt Gerber, one of the employees that worked for me at Metropolitan Properties and I purchased some property at Hnausa on Lake Winnipeg, which we cleared (the boys and I mostly), subdivided it into five lots and sold them. We then divided the monies between Matt and me.

Del got a job waitressing in 1978, and during that summer I heard about a job flying over in Saudi Arabia for a company that was drilling for water. They were offering a lot of money to have someone fly their people from place to place all over Saudi Arabia checking on the water wells and also looking for water. The company was willing to include a nice house in an enclosed compound, and the children would be able to attend excellent private English speaking schools while we were there. As I mentioned, Del was waitressing, when she came home that evening, the four children ran out to meet her and tell her that we were going to move to Saudi Arabia. She didn't say anything, just raised her eyebrow and looked at me and said, "Oh"?

The kids were excited about this possible new adventure, but I thought maybe I should look into it just a little more. First of all, we would be in a foreign country whose laws are much different than ours in Canada or even the U.S., and I would have my family with me. Then I found, that Del would not be allowed to drive a car outside of the compound and if we did leave the compound as a family, she and the girls would have to be covered from head to toe with only their eyes showing.

I then decided to talk to a friend of mine, whose brother had gone to Saudi Arabia to work three or four years previous to get some information on the country and how his brother liked it there. He told me that he had not spoken, nor heard from his brother since he had left. My friend said that he really didn't know what might have happened to his brother, but he was quite worried about him. After hearing that and thinking about it a little more, I decided, that the job wouldn't be the best idea for myself or my family. So I turned it down.

September of that same year, Del got a job working for P. Lawson Travel, a job she really liked. The following spring, she got a great deal through the agency where she was working, that would allow us to go to Germany. A place I had always wanted to see. She booked an airfare for us with WardAir airlines, this was a charter to Germany for fourteen days. So we started planning and getting ready to go. I rented a Volkswagen camper for our use while we were there, and we also took along our six-man Eureka tent and air-mattress, (yes, we were going to Germany, but I still had to keep a close eye on our finances). Since it was the end of June, I figured we could save a little money by camping. I also made a reservation at a "campinplatz" (campground) in Pfronten, (Bavaria) Germany the town where my mother had been born and raised and where I still had relatives.

Del wrote a letter to a relative of my mother's that we had kept in some of Ma's papers which I had in a file, to let them know that we would be coming over and would like to meet them. We didn't hear back from anyone, but we were going to Germany, what else was there to say!!

We picked up our camper in Frankfurt, Germany, "loaded up" and with our German map, we were on our way. When we arrived at the campground, and got set up, we went over to the washroom (which also had the showers) as well as an enclosed lunch room with picnic tables and benches. A lot of people were in there, and a pay phone was on the wall. I asked, if anyone spoke English, and if anyone there knew Frank Erhart? I told the people that we were from Canada, and that Frank Erhart was my mother's brother. All of a sudden, everyone started talking at once, and then someone else was on the pay phone, and very soon we were surrounded by my mother's relatives and my cousins. Wow! Now none of us could speak any German, and there were only one or two in the place that spoke English. But boy, it was still exciting.

For the next two weeks, we got acquainted with my German relatives and had a chance to see my mother's childhood home as well as lot of Bavaria. I even had a chance to meet a few of my uncles who were still alive, and saw the castle that my mom had worked in as a girl. She was in her teens and had worked as a cook's helper at the Neuschwanstein Castle. Ma, even told me that she saw King Ludwig everyday that she worked there. She said she thought he was quite a man, because he would stop and pick-up after the horses in the streets of the castle and grounds.

This was one of the last times that all four of our children were able to travel with us, as the following year, "Butch"; the oldest boy got a job for that summer.

While I was working for Metropolitan Properties, I needed to have the fuel cells (rubber bladder type gas tanks) for my Aztec repaired and that was the start of something new, Hartwig Aircraft Fuel Cell Repair was "born".

Figure 104: The Neuschwanstein Castle where my mother worked as a cooks helper when she was a girl.

Figure 105 & 106: Some of my cousins
in Germany that we met. (Note: the
nose of our Volkswagen camper.)

Figure 107: A view of Phronten Kapple, Germany. (this is in the Bavarian Alps), and is located in a valley of the surrounding moun-
tains. (Note the "Brown" cows) intfore-

Chapter Twenty-Six

Fueled and Ready to Go Again

As I mentioned before, I needed to have my Aztec fuel cells repaired, so I started checking for someone who was doing this type of work, but I could not find anyone. I went back through my records and located the companies that I had used before, to get materials to repair the fuel cells back in the early 1950's. They told me that they were still using the same materials and adhesives, so I ordered some, removed the tanks from my airplane and "set-up" a place in the attached garage on our house and started to work on my Aztec bladder tanks. It wasn't long before the word got around and pretty soon, I found that I had several other pilots with airplanes that wanted work done on their airplane tanks (fuel cells), and we were up and running!

I continued working at Metropolitan Properties, but would work on the fuel cells in the evenings and weekends. Finally I was getting so many fuel cells to work on, that my garage area became too small and I had to look at renting a larger place. I found a small shop at the Winnipeg International Airport in Hangar T-4.

In 1981, I registered Hartwig Aircraft Fuel Cell Repair as a sub-division of Del's business, Hartwig Wilderness Adventures and Travel Service, and I applied for and received our Canadian Aircraft Repair Station License so we could legally repair aircraft gas tanks.

After moving to Hangar T-4, the two boys asked if they could get a job working there for me part time. So I taught them how to do the work, also around this time, my brother Carl, who was painting and laying flooring for me in the houses at the CF base. Was finding that he was having trouble kneeling on his knees, doing flooring, and could not paint during the winter months. He needed a job, so I hired him, and also

194

taught him how to repair fuel cells.

Part of the cost of starting up and running any business is advertising. This meant, putting ads in all of the major aircraft magazines, such as Trade-a-Plane, and different Alaskan flying magazines as well as some others. I also booked a few trade shows. The idea is to "get your name out there" and to become known. I had to have my brother do most of these, as I was still working at Metropolitan Properties and the boys were still in school.

The "repair business" was not making any money at that time, in fact just the cost of the advertising alone, exceeded any and all money that was coming into the business for the first five years. And there was wages and other expenses regarding the business that still had to be paid. That meant, that all the money I received from my job at Metropolitan Properties, except what I needed for my family, went into the business.

I do have to tell you, that no matter how "tight" the money got each month, I would still take twenty percent of what I made from my job at Metropolitan and put it into an RRSP (this is a retirement fund through the bank), I did this, because I knew that I would not get any other money for my retirement years, also I did not have to pay income tax on the first twenty percent of my total income.

I also have to tell you how Del and I tried to "save a buck or two" on food for the family, and my brother who was staying with us at the time. Right next door to Metropolitian Properties office and shop, was a supermarket, they would throw out food (meat, bread etc.,) that had reached the "expiration date", the food was still good, but the store legally could not sell it. I would "retrieve" it out of the dumpster and put it into the fridge/freezer I had in my office, and then I would take it home and Del would put it in our freezer at the house. She would take it out, thaw and use it when she needed it. Any fruit or vegetables I brought home, she would look over and make use of them accordingly. Most of the fruit was as good as new, with only a bit of it that was not, and these she would dispose of. I have to say, that this saved us a lot of money, which I then could use for the business.

Another thing we did was buy one gallon of whole milk a bag of pow-dered milk and mix the two together. This gave us then two gallons of two percent milk for the children. We could purchase canned meat (Klik) at the wholesaler, where I had kept an account when we sold the camp, Del would make "meat spreads" for the children's and our sandwiches and along with her baking, the soups and stews, we were able to eat quite well.

By around 1982 we again needed more space, so I rented a shop on Ser-geant Avenue and again had to build work benches etc., and get this building ready for our use. Then my brother wanted to have an apart-ment to live in rather than living with us at our home on Henderson Highway. So the next project I had, was to build an apartment for him over this new repair shop.

Around this same time, I was looking for a chance to bring my Aztec closer to Winnipeg (I had been keeping it at the Steinbach Airport in a rented hangar). Whenever I wanted to use it or work on my plane, I had to go to Steinbach, which is an hour away from Winnipeg, making it a little inconvenient to say the least. One day I was at St. Andrews Airport and I saw a hangar for sale, I stopped and got the phone number and gave a call. I purchased that hangar around 1985 and flew my Aztec to the St. Andrews Airport and parked it in the hangar.

I also realized that it would make a real good place to expand the fuel cell repair business, so I started working on it. It was just a large open build-ing when I bought it, and needed to be made ready to "house" a business. I dry walled, put in running water, test benches, work benches (both sta-tionary and movable), electrical outlets, base board heating, ceiling lights, an air conditioner, a sewer system and drilled a water-well. I painted the inside, made a storage area for extra tanks, had the parking lot and drive-way paved, and a sign made with our name on it, and bought a very large air compressor. Then we moved Hartwig Aircraft Fuel Cell Repair in, and were ready to go.

That summer we also started displaying at Oshkosh, so I booked a space and flew the family down to Oshkosh in my Aztec, along with two tents, air mattresses, sleeping bags and all of our camping gear, (we dry-camped by our airplane for a couple of years). We also had a display booth, table and literature in our load. I, "Butch", Erich and Del went over and set up and then had a chance to look around.

Figure 108:
The new shop
at St Andrews
Airport.

Figure 109:
Employees in
the new shop.

Figure 110: Our booth at Oshkosh Fly-in.

The following year, I built an addition on to the main hangar, which would then have three offices, a lunch room, bathroom, and a couple of years later on, I added a three bedroom apartment above the offices. Some years later after our son was married, "Butch", his wife and then small growing family would move into, and there they would live for several years until they bought a house.

I also would fly all the "shop staff" to Gods Lake for a fishing trip; and we would stay in a cabin which was owned by my friend, Gilbert Burton near his home at Gods Lake Narrows. This I did every fall for a few years.

Figure 111: The "crew" at God's Lake on the annual fishing trip. ("Butch" has the white cap and Erich the dark

Figure 112: Al with Erich and the "boys" with the days catch.

Figure 113: Erich on "shore lunch" duty.

Del and I were now doing more trade shows during my holidays, but the largest trade show I booked for us to do, was the EAA Air Show in Oshkosh, and we were now starting to get more repair business from both Canada and the U.S.

Our oldest son, "Butch" got married in 1988; he and our son Erich were now working full time in the fuel cell shop. My brother, Carl who had been working for me in the shop, left that fall to go back to the U.S. I was still working at Metropolitan Properties, and would remain working there until 1996 when I left, and then I would start working full time in the "repair" business. But, I had always kept active in the fuel cell business, by doing the books, and the advertising as well contributing part of my wages every month, until I left Metropolitan Properties.

In the fall of 1988, Del and I decided to take a trip to Europe where we would "back-pack" through several countries: Germany, Italy, Greece, France, England, Scotland and Wales. We were gone for a whole month. This was one of the few times that Del and I actually did something that was not work related!

In August of 1989, I was considering opening a fuel cell repair shop in Alaska, as there are probably more private airplanes up there than there are in all of Canada. So I flew "Butch", his wife at the time, Del and myself to Anchorage in the Aztec, and we started to look over the situation and what exactly would be involved. However, "Butch's" wife really did not want to move away from Winnipeg, and since the cost of starting a new shop up there would be so expensive, that it was unthinkable doing it without someone I knew and trusted. So I "scrapped" the idea.

Also in the 1990's, I started another business. This one was buying and selling used cars, "Hartwig Auto Sales". I went to the auctions, found cars, bought and then sold them.

Our oldest daughter, Karla finished college, and in 1989 started working at the St. Andrews Shop where she worked until the fall of 1994. Our son, "Butch" and his wife gave us our first grandchild, a boy, and that fall, "Butch" and I went to South Dakota on an antelope hunt. "Butch" liked to feed his family the more healthful meat of wild game. Plus he also enjoyed hunting, especially with a bow and arrow.

In 1992, I had the opportunity to purchase the American Legion in Hallock, Minnesota. I asked the two "boys", which one wanted to move down there and run that shop. Erich said, that since he was not yet married, he would do it. So I purchased the "Legion" and started to transform it into a fuel cell repair shop. Again I had to put in a test bench, work benches, both (stationary and movable), electrical wiring, windows (as there were no windows in it), an air compressor, a storage area for extra tanks and have a sign made for the new shop. Then I got in contact with a couple of our suppliers to "stock" tanks. While I was working on the new shop in Hallock, I also bought a house for Erich to live in down there while he was running the new shop. "Butch" took over running the shop at St. Andrews Airport.

One day when I was out at the fuel cell shop at St. Andrews Airport, as I was leaving, I noticed that there was an auction going on across the "road". I figured I should go over and take a look. When I got there I found out that all the buildings, which included a hangar and a separate two story office building, "were up" for auction. All the bids that were coming in, were all very low. So I called out, "I bid ten thousand dollars", all at once everyone was saying that they could not go any higher unless they could make some phone calls to their offices for advice. I called the auctioneer on this, and said it would not be legal, this was an auction and I had the highest bid. The auctioneer had to agree with me, and I soon found myself with a new hangar and storage building. This was Great!

Figure 116: Al working on the addition of the new offices and lunchroom.

I could now move my Aztec and a Beechcraft Musketeer into this new hangar and expand our main shop across the road, making it larger.

Figure 117: Al's Musketeer with the Aztec in front of the hangar.

January of 1993 saw the birth of our second grandchild, "Butch" and his wife had another son, and our daughter Karla married Kevin Moore in Las Vegas that June.

In the fall of 1993 our second son, Erich got married. He and his wife Sheri, made their home just below the Canadian Border in Hallock, Minnesota and Erich then began running the U.S. Division of Hartwig Aircraft Fuel Cell Repair.

That same fall, "Butch" and I again went on a hunting trip, this time it was up to Alaska, and we were hunting for Caribou. I flew us to Anchorage, and then we flew out to Lake Clark, where we were flown by seaplane to the hunting range near King Salmon, Alaska. Both of us were successful and we then had to clean, skin and "pack out" the meat to the "pick-up" point. When we got back to Lake Clark, we decided to do little fishing as the meat was being cut up, before we had to fly back to Anchorage and home.

That next spring I talked Del into flying up to Alaska with me to go fishing at Lake Clark, which is around one hundred air miles west of Anchorage, Alaska. We rented a cabin and took everything else including a Zodiac rubber boat and motor and went out fishing for five days. We then flew back to Anchorage where we rented a Class C, motor home and did some sight-seeing.

Figure 114 & 115: Al and Del in Alaska, grayling fishing.

Back in Winnipeg, I was once again back on the job, inspecting the homes at the CF-Base, making arrangements to have the houses painted, new hot water tanks installed and all of the "little" things that were needed in the upkeep of the four hundred and fifty houses that were out there. Also, I was back making sure I had things ready for our bookkeeper so we could pay our income taxes for the business, and was very pleased to see that the company was now in the "Black".

FINALLY, FINALLY, FINALLY!!!! It was almost five years to the day that our income now exceeded our expenses.

In the beginning I used most of my Metropolitan Properties wages, to cover the bills and employee wages for Hartwig Aircraft Fuel Cell Repair and to cover any and all the other expenses.

But finally we were in the "black" and were now able to "put" money into the "fuel cell" business bank account.

We are now one of the largest facilities repairing aircraft gas tanks in North America. My theory has always been, to advertise like a large successful business right from the beginning, as it is this that always "pays-off," and will make your business a success. Our advertising expenses exceeded our entire gross income for the first five years of our business. Now my "theory" was paying off.

Chapter Twenty-Seven

Still Going Strong

Again the EAA Fly-in at Oshkosh was coming up the end of July of 1994, so I had to get our twenty-six foot Executive Motor Home packed and ready to go. I had to take the booth tables apart, and I would put them under the carpeting inside and the booth and all of the "hand-out" literature and stools were stored in the bathroom tub, and the rest of the curtaining and parts for the booth, and any tools that I would need were packed under the table, and we were ready to exhibit. Del was in charge of getting our clothes and personal items and food together.

Figure 118: The "Old" Executive motor home in Oshkosh at the trade show.

We were parking at the family home of Carl Sosnoski in Oshkosh, who opened his yard for people to rent space and park their motor homes, for us, it was the closest to the exhibitor gate where we had to enter. He and his other three brothers also operated a "tented outdoor restaurant", where people could buy food and beverages.

This year also saw our youngest daughter, Colleen getting married and her husband, Jim coming to work for us. I have to tell you that of all of our children only Colleen did not work for the family fuel cell repair business, instead she decided to go her own way and become a nurse. Hey, everyone should have a nurse or doctor in the family, and she WAS continuing the practice of "medicine", a profession my grandfather and uncles had been in. It was only my father who "broke the mold" and changed things.

Speaking of my father, I might as well tell you how it came about that my Dad wasn't a doctor like his father and brothers. Well, you see, my Dad stood six feet, seven or eight inches tall and weighted two hundred and fifty pounds as a young man. He started in medical school studying to become a doctor like his father and brothers, the same as all the generations before him. However, he had a professor who kept harassing him about his size and one day, Dad could not take it anymore and he "hit" that professor and broke his jaw. Needless to say, my Dad got "kicked" out of medical school and he was so afraid of his father (my grandfather) that he "ran off" out west. So, like I said, my father changed things or who knows, maybe I would have ended going into medicine. Ahhh- No!

Back home, we were anxiously awaiting the coming of our third grandchild, who made her appearance in November of that year.

The St. Andrews Airport fuel cell shop was doing well and growing each year and the U.S. Division in Hallock was underway, Erich was busy. That summer after doing the Oshkosh show, I and Del happened to see one of my older half-brother Max's son, John who was in need of a job and a place to live. So I hired him, (you take care of, family first) to work for Erich, I also found an apartment for him to live in, and moved him to Hallock, Minnesota.

Okay, 1996 arrived and I was now able to retire from Metropolitan Properties and I could get more involved in the fuel cell business, (you know, besides the books, advertising and all the maintenance for our different shops)? I could now do more trade shows and Mechanic Seminars (I could only do the large shows such as the EAA at Oshkosh), now I could look into adding a few more shows, to try and increase the business through more direct exposure to the aircraft owners and the mechanics themselves.

Figure 119: The new U.S. shop in Hallock.

Figure 120: Erich and John Kainz working in the shop.

In late summer of that year, I and Del along with Erich and Sheri, flew up to Alaska and had a great time holidaying together. We were able to rent a Class C, motor home and traveled up to Denali National Park. We also traveled up to Fairbanks, Alaska. While we were there, Erich and I looked into the Alaska trade shows, both those in Anchorage and in Fairbanks. I decided that these shows we should also be doing.

Figure 121: Al, Del, Erich & Sheri in Alaska.

Figure 122: The Class "C" motor home we rented. Al is looking out the driver's window.

Our Hartwig "clan" expanded a little more with three new additions in 1997. Karla had another girl that year, along with Erich and Sheri, while Colleen, our youngest daughter, had a boy.

Erich and Sheri needed more room with their new baby girl, so I started looking into plans for an expansion onto his house. We got someone to dig a hole for his basement and built forms to hold the cement for the basement walls that fall.

Figure 123: Al and Erich working on the new addition to Erich and Sheri's house.

Figure 124: The finished house.

The following year of 1998 and 1999, I along with Erich's help, I started getting the lumber, and began building the addition onto their house. Which, if I do say so myself, turned out "pretty dang good"!

In 1999, Karla, our oldest daughter gave Del and I another grandson, this was the third child for Karla and her husband, Kevin. Also that year, we hired Jennifer Davidson as secretary (she is still with us), Del and I were now "working" more Mechanic Seminars and Trade Shows.

The millennium year, 2000 gave us several new Mechanic Seminars to display at, such as the Bozeman AME show, San Jose, California AOPA, Fargo, North Dakota AME, St. Paul, Minnesota and another big one,

Sun & Fun Fly-in Trade Show in Lakeland, Florida, which now gave us a little more exposure and got our name, Hartwig Aircraft Fuel Cell Repair out there as well. We also started doing the shows in; Vancouver, Edmonton, Calgary and Toronto as well as Montreal. Colleen's husband Jim began doing the Canadian shows, and Kevin, Karla's husband began working for us (although he only worked for us for a few years).

While I'm thinking about it, I have to say, if you are ever driving a motor home and have to gas it up, make sure you have the keys with you when you get out. Del and I were heading down to Oshkosh to do the "show", and I stopped at a "truck-stop" just east of Superior, Wisconsin to gas it.

Well, I got out, left the keys in the ignition and proceeded to gas-up. Del had gotten out at the same time to go inside and use the washroom, when I went to pay for the gas, I realized that the keys and my wallet were inside the motor home, and the door was locked!! So, I had to borrow a ladder from the service station and "crawl" in the side window on the driver's side to get in, get the keys, my wallet and go and pay for the gas. To say this was a little bit embarrassing is to say the least.

That year, Kevin and Karla went to Oshkosh with us, where Kevin helped with the show. We were doing so many shows now, that we had to have several other people, helping do the extra ones, especially here in Canada. Erich and "Butch" also were starting to do some of the trade shows besides Del and me. That year, also gave us two more grandchildren, a girl born to Colleen and Jim, and Erich and Sheri had their second child another girl born on Labor Day in September. This now gave us a grand total of nine grandchildren to add to the Hartwig "clan".

Chapter Twenty-Eight

Some Additions to Our Fleet

When the year of 9/11, (this was in 2001), Del and I were again in Florida doing the Sun & Fun Fly-in show and we were also "booked" to do the Toronto Show, (we were doing around seventeen shows a year now), and since there was a little time between Florida and Toronto, we decided to do a "little sightseeing". We ended up in New York City, so we saw all the major sightseeing places, the Statue of Liberty, Ellis Island, and Central Park. While in New York, we also went to see the "Twin Towers", in fact, we took the elevator to the top and had a good view of the New York City from there.

Figure 125: Del in the "booth" at Oxnard, California.

We then continued on to Toronto to do that trade show, (we were using the Hurricane motor home at that time), we had just parked, and were going to relax a little bit before "setting up" for the show which started the next day. Anyway, I am not sure exactly how it happened, but Del walked into the motor home dinette and broke the little toe on her right foot. It was sticking out to the side and she was yelling for me to do something. Well, there wasn't too much I could do for a broken toe, but I "grabbed" a box of band aids, picked up her foot and moved her little toe back until it was straight and wrapped her foot up with the band aids.

Of course, her foot swelled- up and she could only stay in the motor home, while "I" had to do the Toronto trade show by myself.

When we got home, and were out at the office one day, we heard about the "attack" on the "Twin Towers", we were "shocked", after all, we had been inside of those towers just a couple of months previous in June. One of the employees "ran" and brought back a television, and the staff and us watched in horror to see exactly what had happened.

That same fall, in September, our company was booked to do a trade show in Mobile, Alabama and Del and I were going to fly the Aztec down there with the booth and do the show, but because of the attack on the "Twin Towers" we were not able to use our own airplane, and had to book an airline seat instead.

The trip down to Mobile was a real adventure, the Air Canada flight was supposed to go to Chicago and then a direct flight to Mobile. Instead, after we left Chicago, we ended going to Atlanta changing planes several times, and then back to Mobile, but I have to say, we were lucky that we got everything, clothes, booth and literature; of course Customs REAL-LY went through Everything!!

Figure 126: Dave and Carole (Del's brother and wife).

After we got back home, we packed the Hurricane with the trade show booth and display literature and Del and I headed for Oxnard, California where we were booked into another show. When we were finished, Del said that she would like to visit her brother Dave, whom she had not seen for many years. So we gave them a call and drove up to Riddle, Oregon and spent some time with Dave and his third wife Carole. By the time we got home, we were "running" into snow and ice which made it a little "interesting" driving, to say the least.

Figure 127: Dave and Carole's house in Oregon with the Hurricane.

In the following year, I decided that we should add two more shows that I had "got wind" of. One of them was being held at a hotel in St. Cloud, Minnesota and the other one was strictly for seaplanes. Since I was an "old" seaplane owner/flyer I figured it would be a Great Show to do. Del was not really convinced, but she was a good sport and went along with me. Now I have to say, she was right, both the St. Cloud show (mostly Ag-planes and "Dusters") and the seaplane show were "busts". One good thing did come out of the St. Cloud show however, (the planes at this show were using metal tanks, and Del "bugged" me all the way back to Winnipeg about why couldn't we fix metal tanks? I thought about it for a couple of weeks and decided that "Yes", we could actually repair metal tanks as well.

That October, Del, who was very involved in the Order of the Eastern Star, a fraternal organization of the Masons, and got a Grand Representative Appointment to the Grand Chapter of New York State (she was sort of a "good will ambassador"), well naturally she wanted to go and I went with her. We decided to take the Hurricane motor home and use that instead of renting a hotel room (it was also cheaper).

213

After the convention she talked me into going on out to New Hampshire, where a guy I knew was repairing Cherokee tanks. He was elderly and worked by himself, and was always about three months or so behind getting the tanks back to his customers. I wanted to see what his "set-up" was and to make sure that we would not be "cutting" into his business if we started repairing the Cherokee tanks as well.

After looking the "operation" over and talking to him, Del again, asked why we ourselves couldn't have a Cherokee and metal tank shop. She said we should repair these aircraft tanks as well; as it would help expand the business and give us diversity. So when I got back to Winnipeg, I started working on a "shed" we had; so it could be converted in to a metal tank and Cherokee repair shop. I wanted it to be up and "working" by the next big trade show Del and I would be doing. Hey, you know what they say about a "great man"? "It's that there is a good woman in back of them who "pushes". Okay, I have to admit it, Del does get some good ideas every so often!

Figure 128: Working on the "new" Cherokee and metal tank shop. (Al on the ground supervising.)

Figure 129: The "Fuel Cell" business and the "new" Cherokee and metal shop.

That spring when we again attended the Sun & Fun Fly-in trade show in Florida, we had the Hurricane all packed and ready to go. Del, talked all the way down to Florida, how she would "really" like to have a motor home that would have LOTS of storage, particularly storage underneath. She said she was getting very tired of having all of our literature, booth, chairs/stools and etc., carried inside the Hurricane motor home.

Figure 130: Al in the booth in Florida at the Sun and Fun Fly-in.

During the show, she would mention it every so often. So, I thought that I would simply take her to see some motor homes in hopes it would "sort of satisfy her", and make her think that I was "actually" going to consider purchasing another motor home. When we arrived at Lazy Days RV Park, (they have one of the largest displays of motor homes around). We sat down and a salesman came in to speak to us. He asked Del what she wanted in a motor home. He asked if she wanted a "slide-out", and what color she preferred. She replied, that the color really didn't matter, as long as it wasn't a "bright" pink, yellow or purple. Also she said, that a "slide-out" was not really a necessity, she was really only interested in a diesel-pusher and LOTS of storage underneath.

It just so happened that the salesman, we had was interested in airplanes and he liked to go to the Sun & Fun Fly-in every year to look at the planes. He and I then started talking airplanes. Finally, he suggested that we take a "little ride" and just look around. We left the office and started towards some motor homes, he then asked, if I would mind if we took a moment to look at a "coach that had just been dropped-off, as the owners were up-grading to a newer model. He said, he had not had a chance to take a look at it yet. So I agreed, and we stopped next to this coach.

Del went inside to take a look around, and I and the salesman walked to the back and took a look at the diesel engine, and the storage compartments underneath. I mentioned that the engine looked clean and the compartments underneath were nice and large. I asked him, what a coach like this would cost. He replied, he did not know, but we could go back to the office and look it up. Del and I got back on the "golf cart" he was using and headed back to the office. He looked up the price, and I replied, that it was too much. He of course tried to convenience me, but I held firm, after all, I didn't really want a different motor home, we had one! I stood up and was ready to leave. Then he asked me to please wait, and went and got the Sales Manager, who came in and again tried to talk me into buying the coach.

I then opened my briefcase and took out the NADA book (this is like the "black book" for motor homes), looked up the cost for that particular coach, and said, I would not pay anymore than what was shown in the NADA book, and got up to leave. The Sales Manager asked me to wait a moment, excused himself, and the next thing I knew, one of the Vice Presidents of the company came in to talk to me. Then next came the Company President who asked me what I would be willing to pay, as they had to go through it completely and check it out mechanically, both inside and out, as well as they had to clean it and fully guarantee it for one year.

Finally, I agreed to give them four thousand dollars above the "black book" wholesale price. Believe it or not, Del didn't say one word throughout the whole negotiations and we walked out with a "new" American Dream diesel pusher motor home. After we left, Del mentioned, that the only thing she would want extra, would be a washer/dryer so that she would not have to go looking for a laundromat and then spend a day doing laundry.

So I took her next door to Camping World and looked over the washer/dryers that were used in motor homes. We chose one and I let Lazy Days know that we had purchased a washer/dryer from Camping World and I would like to have them install it.

Figure 131: The "New" American Dream motor home at Oshkosh trade show.

The next problem I had was I needed someone to drive the Hurricane back to Winnipeg as I was going to be driving the new coach. I was given the name of a man from a friend of mine and asked my friend to have him get in touch with me. A couple of days later, a man named Dan Zinni contacted me, he had driven big trucks and motor homes for quite a few years and agreed to drive the Hurricane up to Winnipeg, Manitoba.

A day or so later, when we went back to see how things were going, we were told that the coach we had purchased had not been "plumbed" for a washer/dryer; (you see, most coaches have the washer/dryer in the closets, ours however was in the main "galley" under the counter). Okay, so they finally found where you install the machine and were going to put it in, as I was looking over the coach, I noticed some damage down the outside of the coach on the passenger side. It was caused by a forklift with pallets on, so I reported this to Lazy Days and said that I wanted the scratches repaired. They made a "deal" with me, to install the washer/dryer free of cost, and I would "touch up" the scratches myself rather than them having to repaint the whole side of the coach.

Now Dan had never been to Canada or even to the northern part of the U.S. so he didn't know a whole lot about the weather and how quickly it could change. Usually, the weather, the second week or so of April is pretty nice, the year 2003 however, was not the case.

We left Florida with very warm weather, everything was going great, until we "hit" southern Illinois. Marion to be exact, and all at once I heard this terrible "bang" sound. I pulled over to the side of the road, got out to take a look at what the problem was, and found that we had "blown" an inside back tire on the driver's side and no one in sight. Where is a State Trooper when you need one? I got back in the coach and went on the CB radio to try to get some help. I found out that there was a truck tire place in Marion, Illinois and there was even a RV camp ground near the highway. So I started the coach (it was starting to get dark) and "limped" our way to the camp ground and made reservations for two motor homes. Had a couple of "stiff" drinks and went to bed; the next morning I along with Dan, went into town to find the truck tire place to buy a tire and make arrangements to have it put on.

A day or so later we were again on our way. When we started across the upper part of Illinois; (between Champagne and Rockford), the wind was blowing real hard and it was becoming cold. The big awning on the side of the coach "popped" out its cover because it was not locked down securely.

I again pulled over to the side of the road and took a look, and knew that I was going to have to go up on the roof in a "very high cold" wind and manually "wind" the awning up. Dan got out to help me and got so cold that I had to loan him one of my warm coats and caps. Anyway, I finally got it back into its cover, locked down securely and got back on the road again.

When we got to Rhinelander, Wisconsin we found that they had had a major ice storm and a lot of snow, to say that this was a real shock for Dan, would be an understatement! And I was wondering if maybe I was being "punished" for buying a new motor home. But we finally got home to Winnipeg and Dan got back to some warmer weather in New Jersey and a good friendship was formed.

Figure 132 & 133: Al and Butch on their 1991 Wyoming Antelope hunt.

Chapter Twenty-Nine

Another New Challenge

During the summer of 2003 while doing the EAA Oshkosh Fly-in trade show, I heard about the death of a friend of mine, Bill Barton (he owned Monarch gas caps and gas tanks) and I had know him for years. Years ago, he had spoken to me regarding "buying him out", but at the time, I was very involved in getting Hartwig Aircraft Fuel Cell Repair operational. I heard that none of his four sons wanted anything to do with the business, so once again; Del started "encouraging" me to go out to Oregon and take a look into the possibility of buying the company.

Figure 134: Al with his Aztec.

Figure 135: Al's Aztec outside his hangar and the new Monarch Cap Shop to the right.

220

So in the early months of 2004, we drove out to do the Pulyallup trade show, which is located almost east of Seattle, Washington. We were using the new motor home and towing our old grey-green Suburban. After the show, we drove down to visit Del's brother, Dave, and his wife Carole, and the rest of the family, who all lived in Riddle, and Roseburg, Oregon. While we were out there, Del, again "insisted" that I go and find Bill Barton's widow, Helen, to see if she had sold the business and if not, what price she would want for it.

When we arrived, Helen came out to see us, and asked where I had been. She said that she had someone who was interested in buying the business, but the man had not given her any money as of yet. So I asked her how much she was asking for the Monarch Company business, and when she told me, I said I would give her cash right then.

Helen, got in contact with the other man, but he still was not able to get any money from the bank. So, she made the "deal" with me. I gave her a cheque to pay all of her bills and a separate cheque to pay for all the STC's (these are papers showing that the FAA has given their approval so that you are able to manufacture and sell a product), plus all of the stock, equipment etc., I agreed to come back in a couple of months with a large enclosed trailer and load everything up.

Figure 135: Advertising for the business.

April came around again and Del and I drove the new diesel-pusher, hauling a large forty foot trailer down to Florida to exhibit at the Sun & Fun Fly-in trade show. When it was finished, we packed up and started to drive out to Oregon.

We got just east of Pensacola, Florida and once again, there came a loud "bang". I got out and took a look, and "Yes", it was another flat tire! This time in back on the passenger side. Del checked for the closest rest area, which thankfully was only about five or so miles ahead. So I got back in the coach and "very slowly" drove to the rest area. I pulled in and parked. I then explained to the person who was taking care of the rest area, my problem and asked permission to park overnight until I could get the tire fixed or buy a new tire.(This was a NO OVERNIGHT PARKING rest area).

I then placed a call to CAA to get help. Whoever was taking care of the call, sure didn't know anything about Florida or motor homes! She did send a company to help with our flat tire, All The Way from Jacksonville, Florida which was almost five hours east of where we were. On top of that the man who arrived to help was only able to remove the defective tire and then we again traveled very slowly to Fort Walton Beach, where we found a place to buy a new truck tire for the coach. We stayed overnight in their "fenced in yard", until they opened in the morning.

After putting on the tire, we figured we were ready to go, and then we found that the coach "leveling device" was leaking, so once again we returned to the tire store where they directed us to a little dirty "hole in the wall", but we were assured that they would be able to fix the problem, and guess what? They really fixed it! And we were once again on our way to Oregon.

We decided that we might as well take the super highways and go up through California. Well? It seemed like a good idea at the time! That is, until we crossed the border into California, and then we were stopped by a lone State Trooper, who wanted to check the combined length of the forty foot trailer and our motor home. He told me to hold one end of the tape measure to the front bumper of the coach and he walked down the side, I had the tape in my right hand and as he walked down to the end of the coach, I "gently" transferred the tape measure to my left hand and because I was facing the coach, I was able to "gain" a little bit, so he let us go with a warning that we were very close to the maximum limit of seventy-five feet, but he would let us go this time, (actually, we were eighty feet long)!

I have to tell you, we did not linger any longer than was necessary to get out of California!!

Okay, we finally got to Oregon and started loading up the forty foot enclosed trailer with all of the machinery, equipment etc., It took us almost two weeks to load up the trailer, but we eventually got everything loaded, tied down, and were now ready to head home. Boy, that was a trip and then some, we could only drive around forty or fifty miles per hour so we wouldn't blow a tire on the forty foot trailer. Let's face it; I had experienced all the "blown" tires I wanted to have for a Very long time. It took us a good week to get back to Winnipeg and I have to say, nothing looked better, than when we saw the shop at St. Andrews Airport.

After getting home, we unloaded the machinery and equipment into the back of the "office building" that I had purchased across the "street" from the fuel cell shop. These had been the flight offices for the previous owner, so we moved in some movable work benches and set up the machines and got ready to build Monarch stainless steel gas caps for Cessna 177 through Cessna 210 aircraft.

"Butch" took the paper work to his office and got ready to contact the FAA in Oklahoma to get Monarch transferred to us. In the mean time, Erich got the "Bumper to Bumper" shop that we purchased a few years earlier, ready to start making the Monarch hard molded plastic gas tanks which are also used for Cessna 177 through Cessna 210 aircraft; and we were ready to add Monarch to our ads and literature as well as "painted" on our booths.

So when the year 2005 arrived we had quite a "slate" of services to offer to our customers at Hartwig Aircraft Fuel Cell Repair and Monarch Caps. We could now repair rubber bladder gas tanks, repair metal tanks, Cherokee tanks, AND manufacture Monarch gas caps and tanks; we had come quite a way since I started working on my Aztec rubber bladder tanks (fuel cells) in my attached garage at my home.

While Del and I were doing the Sun & Fun Fly-in trade show in Florida, I found that I was having trouble with my left knee; in fact it got so bad I could hardly walk. One day, during the 2005 show, a friend of mine, stopped by our booth to ask if I knew of anyone who would like to buy a mobility cart. He said he had two, but only needed one because of his bad back. I handed him my credit card and said, "yes, me"! He immediately said, "No, I didn't mean for you to buy it, I just wondered if you knew someone who might want it". Again I said, that I did, as my left knee was really giving me a lot of problems walking.

As we were on our way back to Winnipeg, I placed a call to a Dr. Briggs, a doctor in Grand Forks, North Dakota who was from Saskatchewan and had practiced surgery at the Mayo Clinic in Rochester, Minnesota. I asked when, I could make an appointment to have my knee replaced." He asked me, how soon I could get there, and he would perform the surgery right away. I told him, that I still had another trade show to do in Oshkosh, Wisconsin, and I would have to let him know.

That fall at the end of September, first of October as Del's mother was in palliative care (she was very ill), I had the appointment for the fifth of October to have my knee surgery. Del and I drove our motor home to Grand Forks and I had the knee surgery. I guess I "drove" the nurses "crazy" as I started walking without too much trouble almost immediately after my knee was replaced. Five days after I had my knee replaced I was discharged, but they wanted me to wait a couple of days to make sure all was well. I was told that I was NOT to drive for a couple of weeks. Del was prepared to drive the coach (actually she was looking forward to it) back to Rhinelander to be by her mother's side.

Of course, I couldn't let her drive the coach out of Grand Forks; I had to do it instead! She kept asking when she could drive, I told her soon. We drove to Erskine, Minnesota and stopped at a "rest area" (so I could rest for a moment) and I informed her that she could now drive, (but I was going to keep my "eye" on her). I have to say, she did pretty good driving the coach, of course it wasn't me, but hey, what else could I do? Anyway, I did let her drive a part of the way back to Rhinelander (just not through Duluth, Superior, Ashland, Hurley, or any other "larger" towns along the way). But she WAS able to drive the coach!

We stayed there until after her mother's funeral before heading back home to Winnipeg and I will admit that I drove home. What can I say? I'm a chauvinist.

Figure 136 & 137: Al and "Butch's" Alaska Caribou Hunt.

Chapter Thirty

Heavy Turbulence Ahead

Back home, we had a little time to catch up on things (I was not that involved in "running" the day to day business now), I was basically doing the advertising and trade shows, you know, it was almost like being back when we had the fishing camp, and I was travelling all over doing sport shows, this time, however, I had Del by my side. That doesn't mean that I wasn't busy working because I was, but now I was more or less just "overseeing" the business.

When the month of March came around in 2006, I was again out at the shops and as usual I was hurrying to some meeting or other. Well this time as I was in a hurrying, I had my hands in my jacket pocket looking for my keys, when I "caught" the toe of my shoe in a small chipped hole in the cement in front of the door to the shop and ended up going "head-first" into the cement, I came away with a large "knot" on the left side of my forehead and was "black and blue" (actually, the color was closer to purple) all the way down my chest.

"Butch" took me to the Selkirk Hospital immediately and they did x-rays and declared that I did not have a broken neck or anything. I drove back home to Winnipeg (forty-five minutes away), and went immediately over to my doctor, who's office was right across the street from our house at the time. He took a look at me (I was black and blue and on Coumadin, a blood thinner for A-fib). I asked him, if he thought that I should get a CT-scan as I had to leave in a few days to make it down to Florida for our first big show which was Sun & Fun Fly-in. He told me that it could take up to three months for me to get the CT scan, the doctor would have to do referrals first). I got angry; actually you could say that I was "pissed"! Del, tried to talk me out of going she said that she, didn't think it was a very good idea going, with the condition I was in, but I was

226

stubborn and said that we were going anyway!

After we got down there, I found that I was having a lot of problems. I even had trouble helping Del set up the booth for the show. She said that I should just take it easy and she would handle the show alone, but I insisted that she have help, so she gave "Butch" a call and he flew down to give her a hand.

Our friend, Dan Zinni, drove to Tampa and picked him up at the airport as I was having trouble driving and I would not let Del drive by herself. All during the show, I was having a "stiff-neck" and headaches , and when they got too bad, I would take one, Tylenol-1 (this is a little bit stronger than the regular Tylenol) I also noticed, that food didn't taste very good and my sense of smell was also poor. I found that I could not do very much during the day as my energy-level was very low and the headaches were worse (I didn't mention this to Del, as she would have insisted I go to the hospital right away). Yeah, I know, what can I say, my "German stubbornness" was again showing.

Towards the end of the show, the air conditioning was starting to "act-up", so I called Lazy Days and made an appointment to have it looked at. That Monday, the end of the show, Dan took "Butch" back to Tampa for his flight home, and I drove the motor home over to Lazy Days so they could look at the air conditioning and find out what was going on with it. I do not know why, but they couldn't find anything wrong, it was working fine, and we moved to Rally RV Park and were planning on "pulling-out" the next day. We took Dan out for dinner that evening to thank him for all of his help. When Del and I got back to the coach, I asked her if the food tasted okay. She said that she found it delicious; I told her it tasted like "dog food" to me.

That night, I found that my balance had gotten quite bad and I had to "hold on to things" in the motor home when I walked, plus my neck and head were really bothering me. Del said, that if I wasn't better by morning that she was going to take me to see a doctor. I told her I just needed a goodnight's sleep and I took one of the Tylenol-1's and went to bed.

227

The next morning, when I got out of bed, I found that I was very "light-headed" and had to "hold on to things" to move. Del said that as soon as I was dressed she would drive me in the Suburban to the nearest doctor. But I didn't want her to drive anywhere, so Del then called Dan, woke him up and told him that there was something wrong with me and would he please come over and drive me to the nearest doctor's clinic or hospital.

Dan, said to give him a chance to have a cup of coffee and he would be right there. About an hour later Dan pulled up to the coach and I started to get out. Del insisted on going ahead of me, which made me a "little bit angry" at her to say the least, and I told her, "to get out of the way", but she was concerned that I would not be able to get out of the coach without falling. We got into Dan's car and he proceeded on driving to Tampa, Florida and going around to the Emergency Entrance of Tampa General Hospital. When we arrived, I found that I could not get out of the car, and had to be helped by an ambulance driver into a wheelchair which Del had gotten for me. It was a good thing, because I found that I could not even walk by this time.

Del got me registered and admitted to the hospital. I guess I was a little belligerent at the time, at least that's what they tell me, I really do not remember. The next thing I knew, I woke up in the ICU; Del told me that the surgeons had removed a "large blood clot" from inside of my head. She also called home to let everyone know what was happening, and our son, Erich immediately got a flight down to Tampa to be with us.

When I was released from the hospital, Erich drove the motor home to his home in Hallock, Minnesota (it had taken us five days to get to Florida, and he made it back in two and one-half days.). Del went in to say "Hello" to Sheri and the girls, but I was not feeling the best, so I just went to bed and said, that I would see them all in the morning.

When I got up the following morning, my neck felt "stiff" and I was experiencing a headache. I mentioned this to everyone, and Erich told Del to call Tampa General to find out what to do. When she did, she was told to get me to a hospital "ASAP"! Erich, took us to Altru Hospital in Grand Forks (which is about an hour and a half away, but he made it in about forty-five minutes or so). We arrived just before the neurosurgeon left for a holiday. He immediately did a CAT scan and found that the "blood clot" had reformed, not as bad as it had been the first time, but bad enough that it had to come out.

This meant another five days in the hospital and then several more at Erich and Sheri's, until the doctor gave me permission to go home to Winnipeg. I have to say, this was one experience, I could have done without.

You know, now that I think about it, I guess my "guardian angel" was sitting on my shoulder when the air conditioner was giving me trouble at Sun & Fun that spring, so that I made arrangements to have it looked over at Lazy Days, or I would have been driving and ended up in "po-dunkville" or worse.

The early years of the new millennium, saw two divorces in the Hartwig "clan". It is always sad to see marriages end, but that is the way things go sometimes.

By now, Del and I had been doing the trade shows full time. Our travels found us using, the motor home, the Suburban , my Aztec and some-times we had to travel commercially to do the shows, depending on where they were being held, how long they were and the type of show. There is a deference between doing a Mechanic's Seminar (which is only a week-end show) and a "fly-in" type show. Sometimes you have to use a small "table-top" booth and other times you use a "full-size" booth which stands around ten feet high.

Another, thing you have to watch for, is if you have to travel commer-cially, is whether you should take your booth and promotional material with you, or if you have it shipped prior to your arriving at the location, (as I mentioned before, we were attending shows as far away as Alaska and Hawaii).

By August of 2007, our son, "Butch" remarried and then the following November of 2008, he and his wife Salonee gave us another little girl ("Butch's", first girl) to add to our group of grandchildren, bringing the number now to ten.

"Butch's" oldest son Alex, moved in with us for a couple of years starting in 2007 until just before he finished high school in 2009, when he moved out and moved in with his mother.

Figure 138: A magazine cover from Oshkosh 1990.

Chapter Thirty-One

More Turbulence on the Horizon

Del started complaining , that she was starting to get a "little tired" of continually traveling doing trade shows, so the middle of January 2010, we left home in the motor home and traveled down to Florida a little early before we had to "work" the Sun & Fun Fly-in trade show.

We booked into a nice RV campground called, The Oaks, it is located just a short distance west of Lakeland, Florida. It was great, the only complaint we had about the place, was we couldn't go swimming, but then, this turned out to be the "coldest" winter they had experienced in Florida in twelve years.

Isn't this just the way things go? The first time we got a chance to take a couple months off; it's too cold for swimming? In fact, you needed to wear a sweater or a light jacket.

July of 2010, "Butch" and Salonee, had their second child, this time they had a little boy, and (he is the youngest grandchild we have and he brings the number of our grandchildren now to eleven).

That spring, Del, fell and broke a bone on the side of her right foot, and was in a cast, and a few weeks later, I was starting to experience severe abdominal pain. "Butch's" second son, Tyler was being dropped off early one morning before school and since Del had difficulty getting down stairs with her cast, she asked me to open the front door for him.

After, Tyler left for school a short time later; I lay down on one of the sofas in my housecoat. Del "hobbled" down stairs and asked me what was wrong; I told her that I was experiencing some severe abdominal pain. She said that I should go to the hospital, naturally, I said NO!

Now I have to say, that Del has only "pulled rank" on me once or twice in our married life (of course when she has, she has been right) well, she again "pulled rank" and called our daughter Colleen, who was working at Health Science Centre Hospital at the time, to come and get me. Del then told me, that I had two choices, I could go with our daughter, or I could go by ambulance. Well, I sure wasn't going to pay to be driven to the hospital in any ambulance, so I got dressed and Colleen took me to the hospital, where they discovered I had "pancreatitis".

Didn't I say, when ever Del "pulls rank" it usually is for a good reason? So much for "retiring"!

The following year, 2011, was a big year for Del and me. It was our fiftieth wedding anniversary. Now it is hard to believe we had been together for fifty years. Anyway, we decided to go to Las Vegas and renew our wedding vows. Del asked her sister and husband to stand-up for us, and then we were all going to have a holiday there. However, her sister and husband found that they were unable to go at that time.

We booked the Little Church of the West (a heritage building, it was actually the first church in Las Vegas) and set the time for two o'clock (the reason Del wanted this time, was that was the time we had gotten married originally fifty years before).

The day of our wedding, Del and I were getting ready to go to the church, when we got a phone call from our oldest son, "Butch", asking if we would like some company? We didn't quite know what to say, because we really didn't know anyone in Las Vegas, but we did say, "ah sure". Well it turned out that "Butch", Salonee and our two youngest grandchildren had flown down to Las Vegas to be part of our wedding anniversary. They stood-up with us, and along with some friends who were there, helped to make our fiftieth Wedding Anniversary very special.

The rest of our children had booked a special room for us at the Venetian Hotel and gave us tickets to see one of Del's favorite shows, "Phantom of the Opera" for our "honeymoon". All in all, it was a day to long remember.

Of course according to "Murphy's Law" nothing can go according to plan, and that is what happened. Six days after our wedding, Del got sick and ended up in a hospital in "Sin City", where she had emergency surgery, and spent a total of two and a half months in the hospital there; (she really and almost died), and that kind of ruined all our holiday plans to say the least. Our daughter Colleen, made arrangements to get us home on the airlines and Del spent the rest of the summer recuperating.

I figured that after all that, we should now start to experience "clear sailing" ahead. Right?

Figure 139: Al and Del celebrating their 50th Wedding Anniversary.

Chapter Thirty-Two

Let's Try This Again

The fall of 2011, Tyler moved in and lived with us through the last couple of years of high school.

The month of June in 2012 saw two of our grandchildren graduate from high school. Tyler, ("Butch's", second son), and Jessica, (Karla and Kevin's oldest daughter). That fall, Tyler started at the University of Manitoba to study Kinesiology and Jessica started going to the University of Winnipeg to study journalism.

Later that spring, my cardiologist suggested I have a couple of heart valves repaired. He said I was in good health and had not had a heart attack yet, and he suggested, that it would be a good idea to have it taken care of.

When I asked him about having it done in Winnipeg, he told me, I would probably have to wait at least six months, as I had not had a heart attack or any problems, and therefore would not be considered a 'top priority".

So I told Del, that I was going to go to the Mayo Clinic in Rochester, Minnesota and try to have micro-surgery done.

When I got there, I was informed that because of my age they really didn't want to do the micro-surgery, just in case they needed to do a more extensive surgery. Well everything went fine with the surgery; but it was after, that things started to go wrong; and I kept getting fluid on my lungs and they had to put me on oxygen while I was there. Our daughter, Colleen, again came through for us, and made arrangements so I could fly back home commercially with portable oxygen.

It wasn't until I arrived back in Winnipeg and was admitted to St. Boniface Hospital, (where our daughter Colleen was then working); that I found out that I had been given a drug called Amiodrone, which apparently I was allergic to (we didn't know it at the time) anyway after spending some extra time in the hospital and a lot of care, I was able to get rid of the fluid (seven and one half litres), and started to feel more like myself again.

That October of 2012, saw us back at the Mayo Clinic, this time so that Del could have her right knee replaced (they told us that there was a two and a half year waiting period at that time, in Winnipeg). Needless to say, we again "ran" into a small problem, Del got a blood-clot under a nerve and had to have it removed which meant she would have to spend more time in the hospital there.

While I was waiting for Del to be released from the hospital, I got "rear-ended" by a Caravan type car, which was being driven by a teenager with a car-load of his friends; as I was headed to our motor home which I had parked in a trailer park near the Mayo Clinic.

I was stopped at a "red" light when I was "rear-ended", my car, which was a Suburban, and a very heavy vehicle, was "pushed" forward so hard that my cell phone and glasses which were in my shirt pocket were thrown up on to the dash, my right arm was damaged and I did have on my seat-belt (I probably would have been injured worse if I had not been wearing it). I do not know exactly, why the teenager hit my car, except I was told that he was distracted.

Finally we were able to return to home to Winnipeg. You know, considering that both of us had not spent that much time in the hospital or really been sick during our life time, so far, I think we were making up for "lost time".

Chapter Thirty-Three

Looks Like Clear Skies Ahead

Well 2013 started out looking up. Everyone was doing great, and it seemed that it was "clear sailing ahead". "Butch" booked a fourteen day, South African planes game bow hunting trip and I was going to go with him. I was really looking forward to it, I even purchased a new cross-bow to use and was practicing with it, (I couldn't use the re-curve or regular type bow as I had some damage to my shoulders), so the cross-bow was the best for me to use. We planned the trip for July. However, in March or April of that year, "Butch" found out that he was not going to be able to go on the trip as planned, as he was going to have a "growth" removed on his left thigh, which he was informed was cancerous.

Figure 140 & 141: The Dries Visser Safaris and Al sitting in a "blind" waiting for some "game to come in".

So he called a friend of ours to take his place on the hunt with me (the trip was prepaid, and you could not cancel or get your money back). I would have very much preferred going on the bow hunting trip with my son, but I have to say, that I still enjoyed myself, and I got my "animals" as well as lots of pictures. It was quite a trip, one I'll probably never have a chance to on again.

Figure 142: Al with his Gemsbok that he
shot with his crossbow.

The fall of 2013, saw me walking our youngest daughter down the aisle again, and as the saying goes, "she looked radiant"! This time, along with a new son-in-law, we also got two new step-grandchildren, which now brings our "flock" up to thirteen. Wow, is all I can say!

The following spring, (2014) saw Del being elected to again serve as Worthy Matron of her Eastern Star Chapter, which meant I was "also elected" to go with her as her "escort". It wasn't too bad just once a month for her meetings, but then she told me that she was also expected to "visit" other chapters. Of course that meant, I had to also get dressed up in my "formal" suit and go with her. The "duties" of a husband are never finished! Oh well.

That fall, our grandson Tyler, decided that he wanted to be on his own, and moved out so Del and I were once again "Empty Nesters". It felt funny with just the two of us alone again in the house.

When December came, the whole family gathered at Colleen and Allen's for a Christmas get together as "Butch", Salonee and their two children were going to go to Trinidad for a holiday and to spend time with her mother and two brothers. Erich and Sheri along with their two daughters, were also going to be away for the Christmas holidays.

The next winter was a mild one for us, and saw us thinking more and more about joining the "ranks" of the "snowbirds" and going south for the winter months. It also, saw Del's father celebrating his ninety-ninth birthday and a few months later passing away.

In May this year, Del and I celebrated our fifty-fourth wedding anniversary, it hardly seems possible that it has really been that long. Also, the months of May and June, saw three more of our grandchildren graduating from high school and getting ready to begin their lives looking forward to whatever their future holds.

I have been painting the back stairs and deck, as well getting the summer furniture out for the season and generally keeping myself busy. Also, I have been working on the motor home to make sure that it is ready when we are to travel; and we are planning to attend the Eastern Star Convention (and will be staying in our motor home while attending).

What the future has in store for me and Del, I do not know, but whatever it is, I know it will be every bit as exciting and challenging as the years that have gone before.

My life has given me many ups and downs and challenges over the years, but I wouldn't have had it any other way.

The End for Now

A LOVE OF FLYING
(Dedicated to My Husband)

When he young, actually
just a mere
lad,
He saw an airplane and knew that
he had,
To be a pilot and touch the skies,
To be in the clouds with
more than his
eyes.

So each free moment he spent 'round
the planes
Cleaning and gasing in sunshine
or rain,
Just for the chance to take a free
ride,
To sit in the cockpit and soar
to the sky.
To feel the thrill as the craft left
the ground,
To just hear the engine's
Full throated
sound.

To feel the smooth thrust of wings
through the air,
Filled him with joy just being
up there.
There in the airplane he was totally
free,
Being a pilot was what he
would be.

He flew all the time, 'til he was one
with his craft.
and knew it completely both
forward and aft.
So up in the heavens high
above earth
Where a prayer could be whispered
and knew it was heard.
There in the heavens he both worked
and played,
Night after night, day after day,
The man and machine formed a bond
for always,
This love of flying 'til the end of
his days.

By: Del Hartwig

Figure 143: Al driving the motor home.

Made in the USA
Charleston, SC
19 September 2015